CHINA AS A NUCLEAR POWER
IN WORLD POLITICS

China as a Nuclear Power in World Politics

LEO YUEH-YUN LIU, M.A., M.L.S., Ph.D.

Assistant Professor, Brandon University, Canada

TAPLINGER PUBLISHING COMPANY
NEW YORK

First published in the United States in 1972 by
TAPLINGER PUBLISHING CO., INC.
New York, New York

Library of Congress Catalog Card Number: 76-181569

ISBN 0-8008-1470-3

To my wife, Shirley H. C. Chu,
and my late father, Wei

Contents

List of Maps

Introduction

In recent years, Communist China has been emerging as another nuclear power in the international political system. Since 1964, it has conducted eleven nuclear tests. They ranged from the first enriched-uranium bomb in 1964 to a nuclear warhead carried by a guided missile in 1966, a multi-megaton H-bomb in late 1968 and an underground test in late 1969. Further, in 1970 and in 1971 respectively, Communist China successfully launched two space satellites. Thus Communist China has conducted a very impressive variety of tests and at the same time demonstrated rapid progress in nuclear weapons development. It is therefore imperative to determine whether Communist China will become a major nuclear power; and, if so, whether that would affect the present international system. The Chinese basic foreign policy objectives, its nuclear capability and its future nuclear development are all important factors to be considered.

Acknowledgements

FIRST of all, I wish to express my deep indebtedness to my wife, Hsieh-chuan, without whose assistance, patience and encouragement I would never have been able to complete this book.

I am also deeply indebted and grateful to Drs G. R. Davy, F. C. Engelmann and J. P. Meekison for their friendship as well as their invaluable criticisms of my original manuscript.

I also wish to thank Mr T. M. Farmiloe and Mr Patrick Meany of Macmillan, who have been most helpful and enthusiastic throughout the preparation and publication of this book.

Of course, I assume complete responsibility for any errors and shortcomings appearing in this book.

L.Y.Y.L.

Brandon University,
Brandon.

1 Present International Political System

THE present international system can be broadly described as a 'loose bipolar system'. The term 'loose bipolar' represents only a very vague and artificial framework for describing the present situation for the sake of expediency. There are no really adequate terms which could be used to describe precisely what the state of the 'international political system' is.

Despite this lack of adequately descriptive terminology, it is possible to isolate several variables that appear to be essential to the maintenance of the present system. Basically, a loose bipolar system is a system consisting of the following actors or groupings of actors :

1. Two major national actors;
2. Two loose camps, each being headed by a major national actor and including other national actors in varying degrees 'tied' to the major national actors. The word 'tie' refers to the military, political, legal and economic relations between the major national actors and their camp members.

Within each camp, there are one or more military alliances such as the North Atlantic Treaty Organisation, Central Treaty Organisation, South-East Asia Treaty Organisation and Warsaw Treaty Organisation, which reflect the military and political confrontation between the two camps.

3. A group of non-aligned countries which are by and large independent of the two camps.
4. One or more universal actors such as the United Nations.

It is not, however, sufficient merely to identify the major actors, it is also necessary to describe the relationships among them. It is only by first isolating and identifying these relationships that changes in the present system can be successfully evaluated. There are basically six 'isolatable' characteristics :

1. The military, economic, and political capabilities of the two major national actors, namely the United States and the Soviet Union, are greater than that of any other national actors in the system. Only they possess the overwhelming military and economic resources necessary to qualify them as 'superpowers'. Their power to coerce and to reward is infinitely greater than that of any country. It is, however, important to note that although there has been a balance of strength and military capability between the two major national actors, their capabilities are by no means precisely equal in every respect.

2. Only the superpowers possess invulnerable second-strike nuclear forces. Thus, if either superpower were to launch a nuclear attack on the other, the victim would retain sufficient nuclear force to launch a retaliatory nuclear attack on its attacker and cause it irreparable damage. Consequently, there is little incentive for either superpower to launch a pre-emptive attack on its adversary. Nor does either superpower need to fear that its adversary's pre-emptive attack would destroy its nationhood completely.

Furthermore, continuous technological advancement has tremendously increased the destructive capability of nuclear weaponry. Because of the increasing costs of the use of nuclear weapons, many writers believe that both superpowers are cautious in their relations with other countries and with each other. In this way, world war has been prevented. For example, Hans Thirring in 1955 claimed that nuclear deterrence had made for the basic abolition of large-scale world war, conventional as well as nuclear, once and for all.[1] Thirring is, of course, wrong. Conventional wars such as the present Middle East 'on and off' war still take place. Nevertheless, a nuclear stalemate does exist between the superpowers. Both of them appear to realise that their nuclear weapons must remain unused; the alternative being mutual suicide. Consequently, neither superpower would manoeuvre the other into an extreme situation out of the fear that its adversary might become sufficiently desperate to use its nuclear weapons.[2]

In the past few years, the superpowers have experienced many crises in such areas as Quemoy, Suez, and Cuba, where they have made threats of nuclear war. These threats, however, were made in a rather cautious manner and none of them were made for aggressive or offensive purposes.[3] For example, the Soviet threat in the Quemoy crisis was not made until the crisis was virtually over and there was apparently no longer any danger of a nuclear war. The threat made by the United States during the Cuban crisis was intended to force the Soviet Union to remove its missiles, which appeared to threaten American security, from Cuba. It seems that both superpowers have exerted themselves in order to avoid an all-out war. As Ciro Elliott Zoppo points out :

> While threats of nuclear war have been made by both Soviet and American leaders in crises or local-conflict situations, the avoidance of all-out nuclear war seems to have become an established 'rule' of the international system.[4]

Similarly, Hans J. Morgenthau correctly observes that 'atomic power, monolithically controlled by the United States and the Soviet Union and keeping each other's destructive capability in check, is a force for peace, however precarious.[5]

3. Within each camp, the superpower has restrained its members. Thus, in the Suez crisis, the United States limited British and French military activity; in the Taiwan Strait crisis, the United States has forced the Nationalist Chinese to promise that they would not use military force to attack the mainland; in 1958, the Soviet Union refused to support Communist Chinese bombardment of the Nationalist Chinese offshore islands, and in subsequent years refused to build up a nuclear force for Communist China; in 1962, both superpowers pressed their respective factions in Laos to reach a settlement. In many cases, such restraints have also been extended to countries outside the camp. Thus, through their efforts, the superpowers have also brought peace to the 1965 Indian–Pakistan war and brought into existence the Nuclear Test Ban Treaty and the Nuclear Non-proliferation Treaty. Their present restraints on those involved in the Indo-Chinese war and in the Middle East war could be regarded as other cases in point.

4.   Perhaps the most important characteristic is that both super-powers appear to be 'conservative' powers. Neither of them seeks drastic changes in the basic structure and relations of the actors in the present system, or the distribution of power.[6] Consequently, no more national actors are to face serious problems in the maintenance of their nationhood. Both the Soviet intervention in Hungary, with its 'invasion' of Czechoslovakia, and the United States 'invasion' of Cuba at the Bay of Pigs, with its intervention in the Dominican Republic, were basically defensive actions, carried out for the purpose of restoring the *status quo* in those areas.

5.   To say that both superpowers have restrained members of their camps is not to say that the two camps are intensively antagonistic and consolidated military and political alliances. 'Around 1947, the world was like a huge piece of land in which the cultivated fields were divided into two empires that faced one another across a tall fence.'[7] But this is no longer true. The increasing costs of the use of nuclear weapons, the lost appeal of conquest, invasion, and the struggle for territory, the decreasing military threat represented by the Soviet Union, the economic and political recovery of formerly weak allies, together with other developments,[8] have contributed to the relative disintegration of the original alliances in terms of tense military, political and economic confrontations. For example, the siding of Albania with Communist China, the liberal attitude of Rumania, and the 'defections' of Yugoslavia and Communist China have not brought severe disciplinary action or direct military oppression from the Soviet Union. Similarly, Canada's increasing indifference toward NATO and its consequent partial withdrawal of troops from the Organisation have not seriously weakened its relations with the United States. In 1966, a study of the U.N. voting pattern in 1963 indicates that many countries which are supposedly in the U.S. camp also had a record of supporting the Soviet position on many occasions. These countries, among others, were Panama, Columbia, Costa Rica, Jamaica, Peru, Pakistan, Trinidad.[9] The kinds of support the camp members gave to the superpower in the General Assembly also varied from time to time. For example, while Pakistan supported the U.S. position on 'cold war and self-determination issues' at the 12th General

Assembly, it supported the Soviet Union's position on the similar issues at the 16th General Assembly.[10] During the period between 1955 and 1967, Pakistan, Iraq, U.A.R. and Cuba have shifted their support between the superpowers drastically (see Table 1). During the period 1955–67, while some countries in the U.S. camp, such as France, Iran and Guatemala, have significantly reduced their support to the United States, some in the Soviet camp, such as Albania, also reduced their support to the Soviet Union to a significant extent (Table 1). These phenomena indicate that the two alliance systems have been disintegrating and that tension between the two camps has been relaxing over the past years.

6.   There are two other actors which have contributed to the fact that the present system is by no means a 'zero-sum game'. The first one is the non-aligned actor. The second one is the universal actor.

(a) *Non-aligned actors.*   The non-aligned actors are by and large independent of either camp : they often shift their support between superpowers according to their interests at that particular moment, without having to commit themselves to either superpower (Table 1). Nor has either superpower used military force or threatened its use to press these countries in joining its alliance system or camp. Thus in the United Nations, non-aligned countries such as the Congo (Brazzaville), Senegal, Mauretania, Burundi and, to a lesser extent, Lebanon, Saudi Arabia, Chad, Gabon, the Central African Republic, Haiti, India, Burma, Libya and Jordan, have given support to both superpowers[11] (Table 1). Such non-aligned policy has tended not only to ensure a country's independence, but also, to keep the country out of larger conflicts and at the same time reduce the danger of involving the superpowers in a local conflict.[12] As discussed below, within the framework of the United Nations the non-aligned countries might even contribute to the easing of tensions in the system.

(b) *Universal actor*, i.e. the United Nations.   Since its foundation, the United Nations has to some extent contributed to the easing of tensions in the international system. Its peace-keeping activities have served as a kind of 'preventive diplomacy' or 'preventive security' agency[13] to maintain peace in many areas

Table 1

Details of the Cold War voting in the United Nations*

	1947–55	1955–60	1960–2	1963–7
Iran	52.1 pro-U.S.	98.0 pro-U.S.	81.2 pro-U.S.	71.0 pro-U.S.
Guatemala	61.3 pro-U.S.	100.0 pro-U.S.	94.8 pro-U.S.	60.7 pro-U.S.
Pakistan	62.7 pro-U.S.	90.2 pro-U.S.	73.3 pro-U.S.	15.6 pro-U.S.S.R.
France	86.7 pro-U.S.	96.1 pro-U.S.	90.0 pro-U.S.	56.2 pro-U.S.
Cuba	89.0 pro-U.S.	90.2 pro-U.S.	97.3 pro-U.S.S.R.	100.0 pro-U.S.S.R.
Albania	*Not a member*	100.0 pro-U.S.S.R.	98.7 pro-U.S.S.R.	90.6 pro-U.S.S.R.
U.A.R.	40.4 pro-U.S.	41.2 pro-U.S.S.R.	48.1 pro-U.S.S.R.	71.9 pro-U.S.S.R.
India	17.0 pro-U.S.	44.9 pro-U.S.S.R.	30.0 pro-U.S.S.R.	3.1 pro-U.S.
Iraq	62.2 pro-U.S.	21.6 pro-U.S.	58.7 pro-U.S.S.R.	78.1 pro-U.S.S.R.
Cambodia	*Not a member*	3.9 pro-U.S.S.R.	33.3 pro-U.S.S.R.	88.0 pro-U.S.S.R.
Mauritania	*Not a member*	*Not a member*	35.2 pro-U.S.	66.7 pro-U.S.S.R.
Togo	*Not a member*	*Not a member*	15.6 pro-U.S.	90.6 pro-U.S.

* 'The indexes used in this study are very similar to the Rice index of cohesion . . . If a given state cast 30 pro-U.S. votes, 20 pro-communist votes, but abstained 50 times, its Rice index of cohesion would be 20 per cent pro-U.S. (60 per cent minus 40 per cent). This study would award it a pro-U.S. stance of only 10 per cent (30 minus 20 divided by 100). Absences are disregarded here . . .'

Source: Frederick H. Gareau, *The Cold War 1947 to 1967: A Quantitative Study*, Monograph Series in World Affairs, vol. 6 (Denver, Colo.: The Social Science Foundation and Graduate School of International Studies, University of Denver, 1969) 7,24,36,55,62,63.

and thus contribute to the prevention of further military antagon-
isms among countries in the international system (Tables 2 and
3). It is in these activities that the non-aligned actors have shown
their specific significance. The roles played by India in the
Korean war, and other activities such as United Nations operation in the Congo, are cases in point. Of course, in a world in
which the superpowers are still predominantly the major national
actors, all these U.N. activities and the contribution of the non-
aligned actors probably would not have been possible without at
least some consent from the superpowers. But at the same time,
the U.N.'s and the non-aligned actors' services are also indispen-
sable. As Inis L. Claude Jr. points out quite illuminatingly

> preventive diplomacy requires not only that the great powers
> consent to be served, but also that the uncommitted states
> consent to serve. The conception of a U.N. operating to assist
> the major powers in avoiding mortal conflict by neutralising
> conflict zones. . .
>
> The record thus far suggests an encouraging willingness on
> the part of the uncommitted states to undertake the delicate
> responsibilities and onerous burdens of preventive diplo-
> macy. . .[14]

The characteristics of the present international system discussed
above (i.e. the nuclear deterrence and nuclear stalemate between
the superpowers; their restraints upon other countries in the
system; the disintegration of the two alliances systems and the
reduction of tension between the two camps; the reduction of
incompatibility and the increase of accommodation among countries as a result of the joint efforts of the superpowers, the United
Nations and the non-aligned countries) all contribute to its
moderation and stability. The present system is by and large
stable, which is to say that there have not been drastic changes
in the basic structure, relations, and characteristics of the actors
in the system. Stability is clearly a relative concept whose defini-
tion is very elusive. According to General Systems Theory, a
system is 'open' or subject to inputs that may in some manner
upset it. It has a tendency to maintain itself in a 'steady state'
or 'stable condition', which does not mean that it is in a state of
'perfect equilibrium', but is a state in which its basic structure

Table 2

Disputes referred to U.N., 1945–65

Period	U.N. settles or helps settle:
1945–7	Azerbaijan Balkans Corfu Channel Indonesia
1948–51	Korea Withdrawal of Republic of China troops from Burma
1956–60	Suez war Lebanon/Jordan unrest Nicaragua/Honduras border Thai/Cambodia border
1961–5	Congo West Irian Bizerta Southern Rhodesia Aden/Yemen border Cambodia/South Vietnam (U.S.) Stanleyville air rescue India-Pakistan war

Source: Ernst B. Haas, *Collective Security and the Future International System* (Denver, Colo.: University of Denver, 1968) p. 46.

and relationships are maintained despite upsetting inputs or withinputs.[15]

There are a number of factors which could lead to drastic changes in the present international system. These factors, among others, are the proliferation of nuclear weapons in the international system, the erosion of present nuclear stalemate and nuclear deterrence in the system, and a rapid strategic nuclear arms race between the superpowers. Thus, how a new major nuclear power would affect the present system will depend on whether or not the emergence of that power would strengthen some or all of these de-stabilising factors. Much will in turn depend on the foreign policy objectives of the new nuclear power.

Table 3

Disputes Involving Hostilities Referred to U.N. 1945–65

Period	*U.N. succeeds in maintaining truce or stopping hostilities*
1945–7	Indonesia Kashmir Palestine
1948–51	Korea
1952–5	*None*
1956–60	Suez war Lebanon/Jordan unrest
1961–5	Congo West Iran Cyprus civil war India-Pakistan war

Source: Ernst B. Haas, op. cit., p. 47.

Therefore a distinction should be made between countries whose foreign policy objectives are offensive and revolutionary, on the one hand, and defensive and conservative on the other.

Much depends on the foreign policy context. (Do the weapons serve a defensive vision and strategy, or a revisionist or revolutionary vision and strategy?)[16]

A nuclear country whose foreign policy objectives are revolutionary and offensive would not be satisfied with the *status quo* and may well seek to change it with its newly acquired nuclear weapons.

It has been prophesied that many will be 'conscious antagonists of a system of domestic and international order they regard as bad or immoral'. When they get weapons they will seek to change this 'bad and immoral' international system into one more to their liking.[17]

For example, a new nuclear power with revolutionary policy objectives may be tempted to launch a nuclear attack on its enemies to win an immediate victory or it may merely apply a 'hostage' or 'blackmail' strategy to force its enemies to submit to its will.

It is in the light of this consideration that the following chapters will examine whether or not Communist China as an emerging nuclear power will affect the international system and, if so, to what extent. While Communist China's impact on the international system may be analysed from at least two perspectives – (*a*) the ends and means of its foreign policy; and (*b*) the fact of its possession of nuclear weapons (i.e. 'it's just another nuclear power') – the emphasis in the following chapters will be on the former perspective.

2 China's Basic Foreign Policy Objectives

TRADITIONAL TERRITORIAL NATIONAL INTERESTS

THROUGHOUT its history, China has regarded itself as the centre of the world. The term 'Chung-kuo' (China) itself stands for 'Middle Kingdom' or 'Central Kingdom', which conveys 'the sense of a large universe revolving around a primary, directing force' represented by China.[1] Proud of their brilliant culture and historical heritage, the Chinese have regarded their homeland as 'the centre of the civilised world'. The large territory, population, common language, and Confucian political, ethical, and social values they share, reinforce their 'great power images'. With the possible exception of India and Japan, no country in Asia could be compared with China, either politically, militarily or culturally. The military as well as cultural superiority and prosperity of the Han (206 B.C. – A.D. 189), T'ang (A.D. 618–905), Ming (A.D. 1368–643), and early Ching (A.D. 1644–700) dynasties further reinforced the Chinese 'Middle Kingdom' assumption and China's presumed influence in Asia. Consequently, China had established around itself a system of tributary states which were expected to be submissive and to pay at least some tribute to China. At any sign of hostility on their part, China was quite prepared to use force to cope with them. China's expeditions to Burma, Vietnam (Annam), Korea, and many northern areas, were cases in point. Although these tributary states, for instance Korea at the time of the T'ang dynasty, had once been conquered by China, they were seldom occupied by the Chinese. During the Ming dynasty, there

11

were as many as thirty-eight tributary states, including Japan, Nepal, Annam and Korea. Through the tribute system and the constant display of its military might, China not only found guarantees of its security, but also built up and maintained a loose 'Chinese Empire' which covered most parts of East Asia, stretching from the Pamirs to Pusan (Map 1), until after the early Ching dynasty, although its relative influence in the area varied from period to period.

CHINA : THE WORLD ORDER – TRADITIONAL MODEL[2]

(1) *Area 1.* This area contained the eighteen provinces, the traditional territories under China's complete control throughout its history, and was the 'core' of China. It extended from the Great Wall in the north to Indochina in the south, and from the western plateaus to the 'East China Sea', covering about 40 per cent of modern China. It presently supports 87 per cent of the Chinese population.

(2) *Area 2.* This area covered the remaining 60 per cent of modern China, including Tibet, Sinkiang, Outer Mongolia, Manchuria, the offshore islands, and many tributary states, such as Korea and Annam. The Chinese regarded both Area 1 and Area 2 as their vital national-interest areas and therefore were quite determined to defend them at all costs.

(3) *Area 3.* This area covered most tributary states along the Chinese border, such as the Liu-ch'iu (Ryukyu) Islands, Burma, Cambodia, Laos, the Himalayan States, Malaya, part of Borneo and, for a brief period, Japan. While all these states were regarded as within China's sphere of interest, they were not as vitally important as the first two areas and China seldom intervened in their domestic affairs.

(4) *Area 4.* This area covered the rest of the countries in Asia, including India, Pakistan, New Guinea, Indonesia and other countries, such as Iran. Although China was concerned with these countries, its influence on them was limited.

(5) *Area 5.* This area covered countries in Europe, America, Africa, etc. China regarded these countries as 'barbaric' and had never treated them as equals.

Of these areas, Area 1, Area 2 and Area 3 were especially

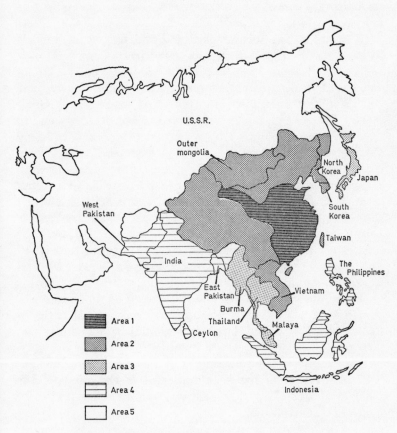

Map. 1   China: the World Order – traditional model

regarded as within the 'traditional frontiers' of China. In fact, until after the end of the early Ching dynasty, China enjoyed its hegemony within these frontiers.

However, during the past hundred and fifty years, China's 'empire' and its hegemony in Asia completely collapsed. Threatened by the rifles and gunboats of the Western countries, China was forced to sign many 'unequal treaties'. According to these treaties, China agreed to indemnify such countries as Great Britain, France and Japan for a large amount of money and to open almost all important Chinese ports to these countries. Many Chinese territories, such as Hong Kong, Taiwan, Kowloon, were ceded to foreign countries. Furthermore, the 'spheres of interest' of these foreign countries were expanded to include other areas in China. For example, France took control of Kwangchow Bay; Britain took control of Weihaiwei and the Yangtze river area; and Russia took control of Port Arthur. Within their spheres of interest these countries had complete jurisdiction. They were, for example, free to build railways and military bases and to exploit natural resources.

During this period, China also lost most of its tributary states. Britain took control of Burma, France took control of Indo-China, and Russia and Japan took control of Manchuria and Korea.

It is because of these developments that a feeling of humiliation and frustration has been cultivated in the minds of the Chinese people. Thus Sun Yat-sen, the founding father of Republican China, said:

> We are the poorest and weakest country in the world, occupying the lowest position in world affairs; people of other countries are the carving knife and the serving dish while we are the fish and the meat.[3]

Today, the Chinese still remember vividly their glorious history and their traditional dominant role in Asia. The concept of 'Middle Kingdom' is still quite real in their minds. Thus, Chiang Kai-shek of Nationalist China maintained in 1943 that the Western countries and the unequal treaties they imposed on China had 'not only rendered China no longer a state, but also made the Chinese people no longer a nation. They completely destroyed our nationhood, and our sense of honour and shame was lost.' He also maintained that the Western countries had taken many territories from China and vowed to recover them.

In regard to the living space essential for the nation's existence, the territory of the Chinese state is determined by the requirements for national survival and by the limits of Chinese cultural bonds. Thus, in the territory of China a hundred years ago, comprising more than ten million square kilometres, there was not a single district that was not essential to the survival of the Chinese nation and none that was not permeated by our culture. Thus the people as a whole must regard this as a national humiliation, and not until all lost territories have been recovered can we relax our efforts to wipe out this humiliation and save ourselves from destruction.[4]

Mao Tse-tung similarly claimed in 1939 that 'the imperialist powers have taken away many Chinese dependent states and part of her territories'. The most important ones he mentioned were Korea, Taiwan, the Ryukyu Islands, the Pescadores, Port Arthur, Burma, Nepal, Hong Kong, Annam, and Macao.[5] In 1949, he promised that 'our nation will never again be an insulted nation'.[6] In 1960, he declared that 'we will strive for eight more years, perhaps ten years or a while longer. Then we will let the world see what kind of people we Chinese are.'[7]

Accordingly, both the Chinese Communist and Nationalist leaders share similar views toward China's past and future – its traditional superiority and its future great-power status. As Hans J. Morgenthau points out:

It would be futile to expect that the new generation will be more accommodating than is the old one when it comes to the restoration of China's traditional domain in Asia. In this respect, Mao Tse-tung and Chiang Kai-shek see eye to eye, and so must Mao Tse-tung and his successor, whoever he may be.[8]

One might conclude then that the 'ideal' world order viewed from Peking is as in Map 2 (p. 16).

Map. 2   China: the World Order – current model

CHINA : THE WORLD ORDER – CURRENT MODEL

(1) *Area* I.   The modern area I includes the eighteen provinces, Manchuria, Taiwan, Sinkiang and Tibet. Territories within Area I are regarded as China's vital national-interest areas and must be defended at all costs. Thus the 'recovery' or 'liberation' of Taiwan remains one of its most important objectives.[9] Also, China considers it vital that Tibet remain as an integral part of China. A third vital national-interest area consists of the territories lost to Russia which should at least be renegotiated, if not regained or resettled. The territories include the Trans-Amur territories, the Soviet Maritime province, the port of Vladivostok, and Sakhalin Island.[10]

(2) *Area* II.   This area covers the border areas of China except South Korea and South Vietnam, as well as Outer Mongolia. In this area, Communist China expects to establish its hegemony and if possible direct control. It is also regarded by China as an essential national-interest area. Communist China's intervention in the Korean war and its deep concern about the Vietnamese war are cases in point. China probably wants Outer Mongolia to be its very close ally if not part of China again. In 1936, Mao Tse-tung said that Outer Mongolia would eventually automatically become a part of the 'Chinese Federation'.[11] Chiang Kai-shek shares a similar view.[12] Recently, Communist China was annoyed because of the Soviet Union's 'turning Outer Mongolia into its colony and military base'.[13]

(3) *Area* III.   This area covers the rest of Asia, including South Vietnam, South Korea, Burma, Cambodia, Laos, Thailand, Nepal, the Himalayan States, Japan, the Philippines, Indonesia, India, and Ceylon. Countries in this area are expected to be friendly towards China. They are at best expected to consult China on all major foreign issues and, at the least, not to be allies of a hostile country, such as the United States. Foreign military forces, such as the U.S. bases in these countries, are highly inimical to Chinese interests and their removal is vital. Nor should these countries themselves pose a threat to China. The recent close relations between the United States and Japan, and Japan's growing military strength, have therefore alarmed Communist China. After accusing the 'Japanese reactionaries' of carrying out aggres-

sion and expansion in South-East Asia in a bid to re-establish their spheres of influence there,[14] Communist China claimed that 'it is a plain fact that the arms expansion and war preparations by Japan's reactionaries are spearheaded against China'.[15]

(4) *Area* IV. This area comprises the rest of the world. Communist China's geographical and political aim in this area remains uncertain. Although it has been claimed that China would sooner or later adopt an expansionist policy toward this area,[16] our discussion above does not seem to support such a conclusion. In fact, the Chinese people seem to have content with their 'living space' since the time of the T'ang dynasty.[17] Thus, what Communist China would do in this area, in so far as its traditional territorial national interests are concerned (*vis-à-vis* its ideological interests to be discussed below), can be answered only by future developments.

IDEOLOGY

In addition to the factor of traditional territorial national interests outlined above, there is another important factor affecting Communist China's foreign policy objectives. This other factor is ideology.

Communist China's ideology, Maoism, consists of Marxist-Leninism and Mao Tse-tung's thought (based upon Mao's experience in the Chinese revolution and his absorption of traditional Chinese tactics and strategy).[18] In its ideology, Communist China identifies three contradictions among the countries of the world :

(1) the contradiction between the socialist camp and the imperialist camp;
(2) the contradiction between oppressed countries and imperialist countries, and
(3) the contradiction among imperialist countries.[19]

According to the three above-mentioned contradictions, there are three types of countries :

(1) communist or socialist countries;
(2) capitalist or imperialist countries; and
(3) countries between these two camps.

In the Communist Chinese view, there can be no relaxation between the socialist countries and the imperialist countries.

> Numerous facts show that, in the struggle against imperialism, relaxation that is won through struggle is a genuine relaxation, while relaxation brought by capitulation is a false relaxation. The so-called relaxation now appearing between the United States and the Soviet Union is only a transient and superficial phenomenon and a false relaxation.[20]

Therefore, as long as there are imperialist countries in the world, there can be no peace.

> It is our view that imperialism is the source of modern wars and that U.S. imperialism is the main force of aggression and war. Unless a resolute struggle is waged against the U.S. imperialist policies of aggression and war, defense of world peace is completely out of the question.[21]

The countries between the two camps exist in a zone called the 'intermediate zone', first mentioned by Mao in 1946[22] and sub-divided into two further zones in 1964. One of these, the 'first intermediate zone', included the independent countries and those striving for independence in Asia, Africa, Latin America. The other zone, called the 'second intermediate zone', included the whole of Western Europe, Oceania, Canada and many other countries.[23] These countries were permitted to remain neutral between the socialist camp and the imperialist camp, but will eventually have to make a choice between the two camps.

In the view of Communist China, 'pacifist neutralism', 'a third road', as well as 'sitting on the fence', are camouflages, and are therefore not permissible.[24] Thus, the Communist Chinese have indicated, in their *Bulletin of Activities*, that co-existence with countries in the 'intermediate zone' is merely a transitional form; socialism will eventually be realised throughout the world.[25]

Communist China further claims that the only way to transform non-socialist countries into socialist countries is by revolution :

> The proletariat world, of course, prefer to gain power by peaceful means. But abundant historical evidence indicates that the reactionary classes never give up power voluntarily.[26]

Therefore, Mao pointed out, revolutions are inevitable.

> Revolutions and revolutionary wars are inevitable in class society and . . . without them, it is impossible to accomplish any leap in social development and to overthrow the reactionary ruling classes, and therefore impossible for the people to win political power.[27]

The areas in which to carry out revolution immediately, according to the Chinese revolutionary strategy, are countries in the 'first intermediate zone'. These countries, because of the frustration and humiliation they have experienced during the colonial period and the enormous social, economic, and political problems they face, are 'the storm-centre of world revolution'.[28] For these reasons, Communist China claims that revolution is ripe in these countries in the 'intermediate zone'.

After revolution has been completed in these areas, the next step would be the 'encirclement' of other non-socialist countries.

The concept of 'encirclement' was originally designed by Mao for China's own internal revolution, in which the peasant class was the most important element. Rural areas are the base areas that will be used to surround the cities in order to complete the revolution.[29] The same strategy is to be applied to international revolution as well. The countries in the first intermediate zone are regarded as 'the rural areas of the world', while other countries, including those in the 'second intermediate zone', are regarded as part of the 'cities of the world'.

As Communist China said in 1965 :

> Taking the entire globe, if North America and Western Europe can be called 'the cities of the world', then Asia, Africa and Latin America constitute 'the rural areas of the world'. Since the Second World War, the proletarian revolutionary movement has for various reasons been temporarily held back in the North American and West European capitalist countries, while the people's revolutionary movement in Asia, Africa and Latin America has been growing vigorously. In a sense, the contemporary world revolution also presents a picture of the encirclement of cities by the rural areas. In the

final analysis, the whole cause of world revolution hinges on the revolutionary struggles of the Asian, African and Latin American peoples who make up the overwhelming majorities of the world's population. The socialist countries should regard it as their internationalist duty to support the people's revolutionary struggle in Asia, Africa and Latin America.[30]

In fact, as early as 1954, Chou En-lai, Communist China's premier, in a report to a special conference of world communist parties held in Moscow, claimed:

South-East Asia, India and Japan are primary targets. The next step is to reach North Africa through the Middle East and the Suez Canal. The third step is to push toward the Sahara from North Africa. Australia is included in the fourth step of the plan.[31]

According to Maoism, 'once the capitalist nations in Europe are severed from Asia and Africa, economic débâcle will surely occur on the European mainland. Then the capitulation of Europe and a universal economic bankruptcy and industrial upheaval can be expected.'[32]

According to Mao, the most important element of a successful revolution in these countries is armed force: 'Political power grows out of the barrel of a gun.'[33]

Experience in the class struggle in the era of imperialism teaches us that it is only by the power of the gun that the working class and labouring masses can defeat the armed bourgeoisie and landlords. In this sense we may say that with guns the whole world can be transformed.[34]

He also points out that:

The seizure of power by armed force and the settlement of the issue by war is the central task and the highest form of revolution. This Marxist-Leninist principle of revolution holds good universally for China and for all other countries.[35]

Therefore, the Communist Chinese define 'revolution' as 'an uprising, an act of violence whereby one class overthrows another'. Only through armed struggle 'can the proletariat, the people, and the Communist party gain their place in a country and win victory for the revolution'.[36]

The strategy of armed struggle is applicable to international revolution as well. The Communist Chinese claim that the task of combating imperialism and its agents internationally is far from completed.[37] They maintain that the imperialists would not collapse by themselves. Instead, they will use armed force to suppress the revolution. The Communist Chinese also maintain that the imperialists are 'a bunch of creatures that will submit to force but never listen to persuasion'.[38] Therefore wars of national liberation or revolutionary wars by means of armed struggle and violence are inevitable. Only through the complete elimination of imperialist neighbours can socialist countries be really secure and safe.[39]

TRADITIONAL TERRITORIAL NATIONAL INTEREST AND IDEOLOGY : THEIR RELATIVE IMPORTANCE

It has long been debated whether national interest or ideology is the more decisive factor in the formulation of Communist China's foreign policy. At one extreme, some observers claim that ideology is not important. For instance, Hans J. Morgenthau maintains :

> Communism only adds a new dynamic dimension to the means by which those policies are to be achieved. In other words, the fundamental fact in Asia is not that China has a communist government but that she has resumed her traditional role as the predominant power in Asia.[40]

Similarly Walter B. Wentz claims that 'communism provides simply a rationalisation of national objectives which existed centuries before the rise of Mao Tse-tung'.[41]

Nevertheless, the validity of this line of argument is questionable. Communist China's zeal in world revolution and communism has constantly and significantly influenced its policy. For example, if mainland China were still under the control of the Nationalist government, it probably would not pay as much attention to the revolutions in countries in Africa, Latin America and the Middle East as the Communist government does. In many cases, such as its policy of encouraging revolution in Japan in 1958 and its antagonism toward the Japanese government, ideological convictions apparently have led Communist China to formulate some mistaken policies.[42] Therefore the importance of Communist China's ideology cannot be ignored. As A. Doak Barnett points out :

> It is true that the Chinese Communists are pragmatic in interpreting their ideology to take advantage of concrete situations and are flexible in formulating their day-to-day tactics. But to underrate the importance of ideology as a determinant of Peking's long-range policy, or to argue that ideology is no more than a cloak for Chinese national interests, would be a serious mistake. The Chinese Communists are motivated by a genuine revolutionary zeal which is probably stronger than that of the present leaders in the Soviet Union. Ideology greatly influences their conceptions of China's national interests, and the Communist belief in world revolution definitely impels them to project their influence beyond China's borders.[43]

Many scholars, such as Morton H. Halperin, Dwight H. Perkins and Alastair Buchan, share a similar view. They agree that Mao Tse-tung and his associates 'probably give a higher priority to ideology than their Soviet counterparts do'.[44]

In contrast to those sponsors of the 'national interest as the sole factor' theory, others maintain that ideology is the sole motivating force in the formulation of Communist China's foreign policy. For example H. Arthur Steiner, and Franz Michael[45] tend to argue that the pursuit of international communism and the mission to spread Marxist-Leninism throughout the world are the decisive factors in Communist China's invasion of India and its close relations with Pakistan (a member of the United States-led SEATO and CENTO). Thus it seems quite legitimate to say :

> If we think of China only as a Communist power and overlook nationalism, we are likely to misunderstand a lot of their moves.[46]

The above discussion indicates that both national and ideological interests are important and both have played important roles in deciding Communist China's foreign policy objectives. As Abraham M. Halperin significantly points out :

> It is sometimes asked whether Chinese policy is based on ideology or on national interest. Neither concept is altogether clear, and the two are not mutually exclusive. Communist ideology is not pure philosophy but also political analysis and strategy. . . While . . . a drive toward great power status has been a constant motive of the C.P.R. [Communist China], it is a motive that has not always pulled in an opposite direction from ideology. . . In a number of situations the Chinese have had options and . . . their choices have reflected both their great power ambitions and their sense of a world revolutionary mission.[47]

Similarly, A. S. Whiting maintains that both ideological and national interests are important to Communist China. He points out :

> The present rulers of China are Chinese. They have lived there, with few exceptions, during most of their past. The environment within which they operate is essentially the same as that which prevailed in China for the previous century. At the same time, they view that environment through Communist lenses. The élite possesses a highly articulated ideology which it consciously proclaims as the basis of behaviour : the Marxist-Leninist creed of Communism.[48]

Robert A. Scalapino, A. Doak Barnett, Harold C. Hinton, Abraham M. Halperin, Morton Halperin[49] and many other writers share the same conclusion.

Both Chinese ideology and national interests are significant factors affecting policy and neither of them can be ignored. In many cases, both factors are intertwined and a distinction is very difficult to make. The present Sino-American and Sino-Soviet conflicts are cases in point. In both cases, differences between the adversaries on points of ideology as well as on items of national interest not only caused conflict but also tended to reinforce each other, thus aggravating the conflicts.[50]

3 China's Basic Nuclear Strategy

As mentioned earlier, many factors in the present international system, notably nuclear deterrence and restraints among countries, have contributed to the maintenance of stability in the system. Neither superpower seeks to change the basic structure, relations and characteristics of the international system drastically. Communist China appears to realise that as long as the superpowers virtually 'monopolise' the world's nuclear weapons, its objectives would be very difficult, if not impossible, to realise. Thus, as early as 1963, Communist China had already said :

> There are more than 130 countries in the world. All countries, big or small, nuclear or non-nuclear, are equal. It is absolutely impermissible for two or three countries to brandish their nuclear weapons at will, issue orders and commands, and lord it over the world as self-ordained nuclear overlords, while the overwhelming majority of countries are expected to kneel and obey orders meekly, as if they were nuclear slaves.[1]

It then said that 'it appears that the Soviet leaders want to have a monopoly not only of nuclear weapons but also of the right to speak on the question of nuclear weapons'.[2] In 1964, Communist China claimed that the policy of nuclear blackmail adopted by the United States imperialists was based on the existing nuclear monopoly and that when that monopoly was broken, the U.S. policy of nuclear blackmail would be of no avail.[3]

From what has been discussed so far, it can be supposed that the Communist Chinese have appeared to regard the breaking

25

of the 'nuclear monopoly' of the superpowers as the first step toward changing the present international system so that their own objectives can be fulfilled. At present, it seems that Communist China could adopt three different, although not necessarily exclusive, strategies to achieve this purpose, i.e. the breaking of the 'nuclear monopoly' – total nuclear disarmament; nuclear proliferation; or development of nuclear weapons.

(1) *Total Nuclear Disarmament*

As early as 1958, adopting a policy similar to that of the Soviet Union, Communist China called for a conference of the heads of the big powers to stop nuclear weapons tests on the high seas and to ban the manufacture, stockpiling and use of nuclear weapons.[4] However, not until after 1963 did it make a complete nuclear disarmament proposal. In July 1963, Communist China suggested that

> all countries in the world, both nuclear and non-nuclear, solemnly declare that they will prohibit and destroy nuclear weapons completely, thoroughly, totally and resolutely. Concretely speaking, they will not use nuclear weapons, nor export, nor import, nor manufacture, nor test, nor stockpile them; and they will destroy all the existing nuclear weapons and their means of delivery in the world, and disband all the existing establishments for the research, testing and manufacture of nuclear weapons in the world.[5]

At the same time, it proposed a conference of the heads of government of all the countries of the world to discuss the above matters.

However, Communist China made it very clear that as long as 'imperialist countries' exist in the world, no general disarmament would be acceptable. Instead, it called for complete destruction of nuclear weapons:

> We are in favour of general disarmament and hold that the imperialists can be forced to accept certain agreements on disarmament through the unremitting struggle of the people of all countries. We are of the opinion that complete and thorough prohibition of nuclear weapons can be achieved

while imperialism still exists, just as poison gas was prohibited. The reason is that the use of such a weapon of mass destruction is completely contrary to the will of the people and would, moreover, subject the users to destruction. However, *universal and complete disarmament can be realised only after imperialism, capitalism and all systems of exploitation have been eliminated.*[*][6]

Communist China's desire for a complete nuclear disarmament and its opposition to any general disarmament including conventional forces are quite understandable. As mentioned earlier, in Communist China's view, revolutions must rely on armed force and violence : 'political power grows out of the barrel of a gun.' Without a strong conventional force, revolutionary activity would be very difficult. On the other hand, if there were a complete nuclear disarmament, the superpowers' nuclear deterrence would be eliminated and Communist China, with its strong ground forces, would have more freedom to act in Asia.

In 1964, after its first nuclear test, a more detailed proposal was made. In addition to reiterating its appeal for a summit conference and complete prohibition and thorough destruction of nuclear weapons, Communist China proposed that countries should promise not to use nuclear weapons unless subjected to nuclear attack. This would serve as the first step to 'the ultimate goal of complete prohibition and thorough destruction of nuclear weapons' :

This concrete proposal by the Chinese government that an agreement be reached first on not using nuclear weapons is practical, fair and reasonable, easily feasible and involves no question of control. If all the countries concerned are willing to make this commitment, then the danger of nuclear war will be immediately reduced. And this would mean a big initial step towards the ultimate goal of complete prohibition and thorough destruction of nuclear weapons. After that, it would be possible to discuss the question of the halting of all kinds of nuclear tests, the prohibition of the export, import, proliferation, manufacture, stockpiling and destruction of nuclear weapons.[7]

* My italics.

In his cable to the heads of government of the world, Chou En-lai also maintained that

> as the first step, the summit conference should reach an agreement to the effect that the nuclear powers and those countries which may soon become nuclear powers undertake not to use nuclear weapons. . .[8]

Thus, after its first nuclear test, Communist China had introduced a new pre-condition to complete nuclear disarmament: the pledge not to use nuclear weapons.

Later in the year, contrary to what it had been preaching in the past, Communist China announced its opposition not only to a three-environment test ban treaty, but also to a comprehensive test ban treaty. In addition, it refused to take part in the Eighteen Nations Disarmament Conference (as it was then called) and a proposed summit conference with only the five nuclear countries taking part. More significantly, Communist China repudiated the argument that the destruction of the means of delivery of nuclear weapons should be the first step toward total nuclear disarmament. Its reasoning was:

> At first glance, such an opinion seems to be not entirely senseless. But after a careful study, it is not difficult to see that this suggestion has a serious weakness. Devils are devils, whether they have long or short legs. Conventional weapons can launch nuclear bombs as well as the intercontinental missile. And ordinary aircraft can carry nuclear weapons as well as strategic bombers. The means of delivery is no longer as important a problem as it used to be, particularly since the United States is working hard to develop small but powerful nuclear weapons. The proposal first of all to destroy the means of delivery in effect confuses the question of complete prohibition of nuclear weapons with the questions of reduction of conventional arms and thus greatly complicates the issue.[9]

Apparently, Communist China feared that in the event of the destruction of the means of delivery, the United States still could have launched a nuclear attack on China. Besides, Communist

China was proposing a 'no-first-use pledge' as the first step toward complete nuclear disarmament. Supporting anything else as the first step would have been self-contradictory.

From what has been examined above, the following conclusions can be drawn:

First, Communist China, after its first nuclear test, no longer advocated a 'complete ban' on nuclear tests, a scheme it had previously supported. Its reason was understandable: such a 'complete ban', if realised, would prohibit all kinds of nuclear tests, including those conducted by Communist China; it was therefore obviously inimical to the Chinese determination to continue its nuclear weapons programme.

Secondly, after its first test, Communist China began to claim that a 'no-first-use pledge' was the first step toward complete nuclear disarmament. Communist China might be sincere in advocating this 'pledge'. For one thing, if the superpowers were to accept its proposal, their ability to apply nuclear pressure on Communist China would be greatly reduced.

There are reasons to believe that Communist China never expected the superpowers to accept its proposal. The United States, for one, has not been very enthusiastic about the proposal. One of the reasons is that the United States currently has many treaty obligations and commitments in Asia. A no-first-use pledge would seriously reduce their credibility to the allies and their effectiveness against possible adversaries. As United States Secretary of State Rusk said,

> the defense system of the United States and its allies, freely arrived at in accord with the United Nations Charter, includes nuclear weapons. This must continue to be the case.[10]

In reply to Communist China's proposed pledge, President Johnson said that Communist China 'fools no one when it offers to trade away its first small accumulation of nuclear power against the mighty arsenals of those who limit Communist Chinese ambitions'.[11] Rusk called it, along with other Chinese proposals, a 'smokescreen' to cover up their other intentions.[12]

The Soviet Union did not oppose the proposed pledge openly. However, it would probably not have accepted it either, judging by its previous position. For instance, in the United Nations, it merely agreed to prohibit the use of nuclear weapons against non-nuclear states parties to the Non-proliferation Treaty.[13] Reactions by other countries were also cool.

Thus, although Communist China might be sincere in proposing this 'no-first-use pledge' and other measures of disarmament, it appears to realise that its proposals have no chance of being accepted. Therefore, it only expects its proposals to serve the following purposes :

(1) Through these 'peaceful gestures' to attempt to convince the superpowers of its peaceful intention so that they would not consider taking any action against the development of nuclear weapons by the Chinese, such as the destruction of their nuclear facilities;

(2) To reduce unfavourable reactions to the Chinese nuclear tests or fear among other Asian countries;

(3) To cover up its refusal to sign the Partial Nuclear Test Ban Treaty.

(2) *Nuclear Proliferation*

For Communist China, the second approach to breaking the 'monopoly of nuclear weapons' and the 'co-domination' of the world by the superpowers is to have as many nuclear countries in the world as possible, so that the nuclear deterrence maintained by the superpowers in the world could be discredited. This position makes Communist China one of the very few countries in the world which openly advocates nuclear proliferation.

Beginning in 1956–7, both the United States and the Soviet Union began to worry about the problem of nuclear proliferation. However, many high-ranking Chinese officers indicated that they considered nuclear proliferation to be desirable. For example, in 1958 General Liu Ya-lou, Commander-in-Chief of the Communist Chinese Air Force, and in 1961 Chen Yi, Vice-Premier and Foreign Minister, both said that the spread of nuclear weapons to as many countries as possible was desirable, for it would increase the prospects of complete nuclear disarmament.[14] Communist China also maintained that, unless the United

States stopped all nuclear tests, every country should seek for nuclear weapons.[15] In August 1963, Communist China claimed:

Did the danger of nuclear war become greater or less when the number of nuclear powers increased from one to two? We say it becomes less, not greater.

Whether or not nuclear weapons help peace depends on who possesses them. It is detrimental to peace if they are in the hands of imperialist countries; it helps peace if they are in the hands of socialist countries. It must not be said indiscriminately that the danger of nuclear war increases along with the increase in the number of nuclear powers.[16]

The Partial Test Ban Treaty of 1963, sponsored by the superpowers, should therefore be, in Communist China's view, rejected because it was designed by them to 'consolidate their nuclear monopoly'.[17]

In 1964, immediately after its first nuclear test on 16 October, there were some notable changes in Communist China's policy toward nuclear proliferation. Before the test, Communist China, although it opposed the Partial Test Ban Treaty, still advocated a total nuclear test ban. However, after its first nuclear test in 1964, it started to denounce such a total ban. It argued that because the United States had already conducted hundreds of nuclear tests and possessed a huge stockpile of nuclear weapons, a complete nuclear test ban would not affect its 'monopoly' of nuclear weapons.[18] Its true motive probably is this: now that it has already successfully conducted its first nuclear test, it intends to conduct more in the future. A total test ban would make this impossible.

After its first nuclear test, Communist China stopped actively advocating nuclear proliferation for a while. But it still claimed that the possession of nuclear weapons by socialist countries like China was desirable:

The nuclear weapons in the hands of China and those in the hands of United States imperialism are, of course, fundamentally different in nature. China is a socialist country. . . Having possessed nuclear weapons, we shall continue to pursue, as we did in the past, the foreign policy of peace. . .[19]

So far, Communist China's position on world nuclear proliferation remains unchanged. Although Communist China might not at present be able to help other countries to possess nuclear weapons, its stand and arguments in favour of nuclear proliferation might have significant impact on many non-nuclear countries in the world and might encourage many countries to develop their nuclear capabilities.

(3) *Development of Nuclear Weapons*

Although Communist China has advocated nuclear proliferation, it appears that its more direct and true intention is to find a rationale for the development of its own nuclear weapons. It appears that in the Chinese view, the most effective way to break the 'nuclear monopoly' and 'world co-domination' by the superpowers is by China's becoming a strong and powerful nuclear country itself. In fact, this is its most important alternative and Communist China apparently has pursued it most vigorously. The next chapter will examine this alternative.

4 China and its Development of Nuclear Weapons

COMMUNIST CHINA's nuclear programme actually started about 1953, nominally to develop the peaceful use of atomic energy. In May of the same year a Committee of Atomic Energy was set up in the Chinese Academy of Science and as early as March 1954 Kuo Mo-jo, President of the Academy, announced that China had laid the foundation of atomic energy research. On 12 October 1954, an agreement to co-operate on scientific and technological matters was signed by Communist China and the Soviet Union. On 18 January 1955 the Soviet Union announced that it would help Communist China to study the peaceful uses of atomic energy, and that the latter was to receive a research reactor with a head capacity of 6500–10,000 kilowatts. In the same year, Communist China announced its first Five Year Plan in which the development of the peaceful use of nuclear energy was listed as the first major task.

On 15 October 1957, the 'New Technology for National Defence' agreement was signed by the Soviet Union and Communist China. In the agreement, the Soviet Union promised China a joint research programme on 122 scientific and technological items from 1958 to 1962. Later reports only suggested that one of the two key fields in the programme was to be the peaceful uses of atomic energy.[1]

The Academy's Institute of Physics was also expanded, and

by the end of 1957 the Institute had more than 200 personnel, including eighty scientists and seventy technicians. It was probably in 1957–8 that Communist China started to develop its independent nuclear weapons programme. In 1958, the first Chinese experimental reactor with a head capacity of 7000 to 10,000 kilowatts went into operation. The first chain reaction started and the first uranium was produced in the same year, with Kuo Mo-jo announcing that Communist China was entering the atomic age.[2]

With Russian assistance, Communist China made extensive progress in its nuclear programme. However, after 1959, the Soviet Union began to withdraw aid from the Chinese programme and apparently decided to discontinue its assistance altogether. At the same time, it tore up the 'New Technology for National Defence' Agreement of 1957 and urged the Communist Chinese not to seek an independent nuclear capability. What is more, Communist China said :

> As far back as 1959, the Soviet leaders made a gift to the United States of their refusal to provide China with the technical data required for the manufacture of nuclear weapons. But for the sake of large interest, we never mentioned this before, not even between fraternal parties.
>
> Not only have you [the Soviet Union] perfidiously and unilaterally scrapped the agreement on providing China with nuclear technical data, but you have blatantly given more and more military aid to the Indian reactionaries.[3]

Communist China also accused the Soviet Union of breaking a promise to provide China with a sample atomic bomb and technical data on its manufacture.[4] Although the Soviet Union denied this promise, Alice Langley Hsieh believes that there was probably such a promise made at the time of the Mao–Khrushchev meeting in November, 1957.[5]

After July 1960, the Soviet Union further withdrew its nuclear assistance from Communist China. Russian personnel, especially those involved in nuclear research, left China for the Soviet Union. Communist China's determination to continue its nuclear weapons development, however, remained unchanged, and it concentrated personnel and resources on the development of nuclear weapons, which it regarded as 'peak science'. In October 1961, Chen Yi claimed that it was only a matter of time before China possessed nuclear weapons.[6] In 1963, he said that China would have to produce nuclear weapons even if the Chinese were so poor that they could not afford to buy trousers.[7] In July 1963, Kuo Mo-jo announced that Communist China would soon break the monopoly of nuclear weapons maintained by the present nuclear powers.[8]

Through its determination and intensive effort, Communist China successfully conducted its first nuclear test on 16 October 1964, on the test grounds at Lop Nor in Sinkiang province.[9] It was a fixed explosion on a 70-metre steel tower. Significantly, it was a fission device built of enriched uranium, U 235, which produced a yield equivalent to 20 kilotons of T.N.T. Apparently Communist China had successfully separated out U 238 to produce U 235. This process is much more difficult and sophisticated than the one using natural uranium to produce plutonium for the bombs, a method used by Great Britain and France in their nuclear weapons programme. This test has two implications. First, Communist China is capable of extracting fissionable U 235 in substantial quantities on a large scale through its gaseous diffusion plant. Secondly, since enriched uranium could increase a country's capability to produce tritium, a basic constituent of thermonuclear bombs, the result of this test suggests that Communist China might have intended to develop its hydrogen bombs. Thus, the British Royal Institute of International Affairs predicted that Communist China might have hydrogen bombs within two to five years.[10] Communist China's later tests proved that this was indeed the case.

In addition, in the first test, a relatively 'advanced' trigger technique called 'implosion' was used.[11] This system is more advanced than the usually used 'gun-barrel' trigger technique and since it can guarantee 'sure-fire', it can be used in war without testing.

On 14 May 1965, Communist China conducted its second nuclear test : a bomb delivered by an aircraft (probably a TU-4) was exploded over the same site as the previous one.[12] Like the first one, this test used uranium, but it produced a yield equivalent to 40–50 kilotons of T.N.T. Since the bomb was dropped from an aircraft, it meant that Communist China had perfected a device compact enough to be carried by aircraft.

The third test was conducted on 9 May 1966, when a bomb was dropped from an aircraft (probably a TU-16 bomber) and produced a yield equivalent to 200 kilotons of T.N.T. The U.S. Atomic Energy Commission speculated that a core of enriched uranium with quantities of lithium 6, a thermonuclear material, was used as a liner. A fission trigger was also used to ignite the thermonuclear material. This test indicated that Communist China was on its way toward H-bomb development.[13]

In early 1966, United States Defence Secretary McNamara estimated that Communist China would soon be able to launch a nuclear attack on countries within 500 miles of its borders.[14] His estimate seemed to be at least partially correct. On 27 October 1966 Communist China conducted its fourth test, using a nuclear warhead on a guided missile.[15] The missile was probably similar to Russia's SS-4 medium-range type. It carried a warhead made of U 235 a distance of approximately 600 miles and reportedly hit the target accurately.[16] The blast produced a yield equivalent to 20 kilotons of T.N.T.

The fifth test was a bomb detonation on 28 December 1966. The U.S. Atomic Energy Commission estimated the size of the blast at 'a few hundred kilotons', probably between 300 and 500 kilotons.[17] The Commission also observed that the test used a triple-stage method in its explosion. Consequently, the bomb was not only very powerful but also the 'dirtiest', in the sense that the output of radiation and fall-out was maximised. Since thermonuclear reaction had taken place, United States experts regarded the test as a sign of Communist China's progress in the manufacture of fissionable material and one more step toward development of an H-bomb.[18]

Then, on 17 June 1967, came the sixth test, which consisted of a hydrogen bomb dropped from a high-flying TU-16. Its blast produced a powerful yield equivalent to three to seven megatons of T.N.T. United States officials were surprised by the speed of Communist China's H-bomb development and Senator John O. Pastore called the test a 'dramatic and upsetting event'.[19] On the strength of the fourth test and of this test, United States military analysts expressed the opinion that Communist China had given priority to its missile development rather than its nuclear capacity. Pressure was also felt for the development of a missile defence system in the United States.[20]

On 24 December 1967, an attempted thermonuclear explosion was conducted. Only the first fission cycle in the process was completed and therefore it only produced a yield equivalent to 20,000 tons of T.N.T. The test was never officially announced by Communist China.

After this abortive test, there was no nuclear test until 27 December 1968, when a hydrogen bomb was detonated. It produced a yield equivalent to three megatons of T.N.T. The United States Atomic Energy Commission confirmed that it was a thermonuclear test.

In September 1969 two tests were conducted in rapid succession. The first one was an underground nuclear detonation conducted on 22 September (by mainland China time, 23 September), which produced an explosion equivalent to 200 to 250 kilotons of T.N.T. The second one was a hydrogen bomb explosion conducted on 29 September, which produced an explosion equivalent to three megatons of T.N.T. Finally, on 14 October 1970, the eleventh nuclear test, which was similar to the last one, was conducted.

These tests make it clear that Communist China's nuclear weapons programme has been carried on at a fast pace. It took the country only two and a half years after its first test in 1964 to explode its first H-bomb. It also successfully reduced the size and weight of its warheads to deliverable form, and conducted its first underground test. It has thus already passed France in nuclear weapons development and may overtake Britain in the near future.

Communist China takes great pride in what it has achieved in its nuclear weapons development.

The first nuclear test by our country surpassed the levels attained in the initial tests of the United States, Britain and France! It took China just over a year to carry out a nuclear explosion containing thermonuclear material after successfully exploding its first atomic bomb. This big-leap-forward speed fully proves that the Chinese people, armed with the thought of Mao Tse-tung, dare to break a path none before has walked and dare to scale peaks others have not climbed.[21]

At the same time, Communist China also stated that it would try to develop technology in its programme.

> If we do not want to follow the old path of the technical development of other countries and crawl after others, we must break conventions and learn from advanced experience as much as possible.[22]

In late 1969, after it had successfully conducted two nuclear tests – one underground explosion and one hydrogen bomb – Communist China claimed that it was making the most rapid progress in science :

> The successful tests of atom bomb, guided missiles and hydrogen bombs one after another in China are eloquent proof that China's socialist industry, science and technology are advancing rapidly. It took seven years and four months for the United States of America to advance from the explosion of the first atom bomb to a nuclear explosion containing thermonuclear material. In two years and eight months China successfully exploded her first hydrogen bomb. Confronted with these iron-clad facts, even our enemies have to admit that China is making the most rapid progress in the world in the development of the most advanced science and technology.[23]

Many western experts agree that Communist China has already made very impressive advances in nuclear weapons development and can produce H-bombs by a comparatively simple process.[24] Many United States officials as well as the U.S. Joint Congressional Commission on Atomic Energy admitted that China's nuclear weapons progress has been more rapid and surprisingly more effective than had been expected or predicted. The Commission's report was based on secret testimony in early 1967 by representatives of the State and Defence Departments, the Central Intelligence Agency, the U.S. Atomic Energy Commission, and many atomic weapons laboratories.[25] Dr R. E. Lapp also believed that Communist China would be able to challenge the United States sooner than U.S. military officials expected.[26]

At present, the Communist Chinese resources known to exist outside official circles in China are as follows.

FACILITIES

There are at least four operational nuclear plants in Communist China. The first one, which is probably the most important, is a gaseous diffusion plant at Lanchow. It could produce uranium 235 with an annual capacity of more than 100 kilogrammes in 1963, when it began its operation, and was estimated to be able to produce about 500 kilogrammes annually in 1967.[27] Its present capacity is probably even greater. The second is a reactor at Paotou in Suiyuan province and was first heard of outside China in 1964. It is believed to belong to the 100,000,000- to 200,000,000-kilowatt class and can produce about 10 kilogrammes of plutonium 239 annually. The third nuclear plant is the Yumen atomic energy plant located in Kansu province. It can produce approximately 200 kilogrammes of plutonium 239 annually. The fourth is the Haiyen nuclear plant on the eastern shore of Lake Tsinghai. It was completed in 1967 and was designed to produce uranium bombs, but the exact products remain unknown. It appears that Communist China has an adequate supply of uranium for its future nuclear weapons programme.

PERSONNEL

It has been estimated that if a country wishes to build installations to produce nuclear weapons on a continuous basis, approximately 1300 to 2000 engineers and 500 to 750 scientists will be required for research and operation.[28] These engineers and scientists would include chemists, physicists, chemical engineers, mechanical engineers, electrical engineers, electronic engineers, radiological engineers, metallurgists, and civil/architectural engineers. Until 1960 Communist China had relied on the approximately 11,000 to 50,000 Russian specialists in China to develop its science and technology. More than 700 of them were intended to help Communist China to establish a new educational system. Furthermore, about 38,000 Chinese scientists were receiving training in the Soviet Union, and many of them worked at the Joint Institute of Nuclear Research at Dubna in Russia.[29]

After 1961, Communist China turned to European countries for help. Chinese scientists visited and worked at European research institutes in France and England. Scientists from advanced countries such as Australia, New Zealand, the Scandinavian countries, Switzerland, Austria and Japan often visited Communist China as well; some of them stayed to help train Chinese personnel.[30] Many Chinese scientists hold higher degrees from technically advanced western countries. In Communist China, there were reportedly 1100 scientists, engineers, and medical doctors with overseas Ph.D. degrees and 5500 others with other degrees in science, engineering or medicine received overseas.[31] Through these scientists, modern scientific methods and technical skills were introduced into China and helped it lay the foundation of a nuclear weapons programme.

In Communist China, many established institutes also conduct intensive training programmes for scientists. Among the important institutes are Peking University, the Chinese University of Science and Technology, the Chinese Academy of Science of Peking, the Institute of Applied Physics, and the Academy of Military Science. It has been estimated that from 1949 to 1960 about 230,000 engineers and scientists graduated from these institutes and 2,000,000 more had done so by 1967.[32]

A possible personnel problem for Communist China may be the lack of senior scientists; although it has already had many outstanding experts such as Chien San-chiang, Wang Kan-chang, Chao Chung-yao, and Wei Chung-hua. Wang and Chieng are now in charge of Communist China's nuclear weapons programme.[33]

NATURAL RESOURCES

The most important natural resource needed for the manufacture of nuclear weapons is uranium. Reportedly, rich uranium ore beds were discovered in Sinkiang province between 1944 and 1949. Uranium deposits were also found in Anshan, Chung-chak, Altai, Kashgar, and other places. Large-scale exploitation began around 1950–1 through Sino-Soviet joint effort, but after 1962 Communist China took over the complete operation.

Besides uranium, Communist China also has within its borders many of the resources required for nuclear weapons development, including the lithium concentrates needed for the production of hydrogen bombs.[34]

EQUIPMENT, INSTRUMENTS, AND MATERIALS

Before 1960, most technical equipment and precision instruments used in Communist Chinese scientific research were supplied by the Soviet Union. Afterwards, Communist China began to import a large quantity of these materials and this equipment from various other advanced countries, especially Japan, Switzerland, Czechoslovakia, East Germany and West Germany. Japanese firms have not only assembled and installed the equipment they have sold, but have also assisted in training Chinese personnel. The materials they have sold to Communist China include the basic components of rocket warheads.[35] The West German firms provide Communist China with electronic computers, measuring instruments for tracking missiles, and materials for nuclear reactors. The Swiss firms provide Communist China with rocket engineering tools and measuring instruments. During 1966–7 Communist China reportedly paid some twenty-five million dollars to Swiss firms alone.[36]

Thus, it appears that Communist China has access to equipment and instruments needed for its nuclear weapons development.

At present, Communist China appears to have given top priority to the manufacture of electronic, automation, and precision instruments, as well as equipment and heavy machinery. Many of its 'Machine Building Ministries' concentrate on the development of radioactive elements and on the electronics, telecommunications and aeronautical engineering industries.[37] Thus, Communist China might even become self-sufficient in the future.

DELIVERY SYSTEM

Delivery capability is an important step in nuclear weapons development. For Communist China, there are three possible alternatives in building up a delivery system : long-range manned bombing aircraft, middle-range missiles, and intercontinental range missiles (I.C.B.M.).

Communist China's present manned bomber force consists of approximately 300 TU-4 bombers and as many IL-28 models. Each bomber can carry a bomb load of two tons. Communist China's fourth and sixth tests indicated that it was capable of reducing the size and weight of its bombs so that they could be carried and dropped by these bombers.[38] It appears that for the foreseeable future Communist China would rely on its medium-range bombers, such as the TU-16, as its major delivery system.[39] However, recent developments also indicate that Communist China has been giving priority to missile development. At first, Communist China's short-range rockets were apparently Soviet-made, but by 1958 it had decided to give priority to the development of its own missile production. It has been reported that as early as 1963 Communist China had already tested missiles at 500- to 700-mile ranges. At present, Communist China probably has two programmes : medium-range ballistic missiles (M.R.B.M.s) and intermediate-range ballistic missiles (I.R.B.M.s) on the one hand, and the I.C.B.M.s, with a range of several thousand miles, on the other. Both M.R.B.M.s and I.R.B.M.s are very mobile and 'could be tailored to a procurement of long-range submarines capable of launching missiles, as well as being launched from ground bases'.[40] The missile used by Communist China in its fourth test belonged to one of these categories, and it is believed that this is the area in which Communist China has placed its emphasis. This conclusion was shared by Secretary of Defence Laird in his budget statement for the fiscal year 1971.[41]

However, Communist China does not appear to have forsaken the option of I.C.B.M.s. To be sure, some authorities have doubts about Communist China's plan to build up an I.C.B.M. force. For instance, in 1965, Morton H. Halperin observed :

In view of the high costs and resources that would be needed to create an intercontinental delivery capability . . . the Chinese might decide to postpone indefinitely the development of an intercontinental capability.[42]

His estimate does not appear to be completely correct. For one thing, even token I.C.B.M.s which could reach Moscow and Washington would give Communist China tremendous psychological satisfaction and a feeling of 'equal power' with the superpowers. Furthermore, as discussed below,[43] its political impact on Asian countries would be very great. Many Asian countries might therefore align themselves more closely with Communist China. Both for psychological and political reasons, therefore, Communist China would probably regard it as advisable to develop its I.C.B.M.s. As early as 1964 Chen Yi had asserted that China was determined to 'catch up' with the superpowers:

> Whatever the leading powers in the world can do, whatever level of technology they have reached, we want to catch up and arrive at the same level.[44]

A recent study in Hong Kong of reports from Peking indicates that Communist China is stepping up its I.C.B.M. programme.[45]

PRESENT MISSILE PROGRAMME AND NUCLEAR WARHEAD DEVELOPMENT

At present, Communist China already has a limited ability to produce and assemble missiles. It has many missile-producing and assembly plants at Paotou, Sian, Shenyang, and other places. The shells and engines of the missiles are produced at the Shenyang Ordnance Factory, Harbin Ordnance Factory, Sian Factory, Kansu Ordnance Factory, and Chengtu Factory. Solid and liquid fuels for missiles are produced at the Liaoyan Ordnance Factory, Taiyuan Factory, Hsianghsing Gunpowder Factory in Hunan, Lu-Ta (Port Arthur and Dairen) Missile Fuel Plant, and the Lanchow Missile Fuel Plant.

Outsiders already know of three Chinese test grounds for missiles: (1) the Paotou missile testing ground, which serves short-range ground-to-ground missiles. (2) The Western Ningsia missile testing centre, which accommodates ground-to-air, air-to-air and ground-to-ground missiles of medium and short range. Reports indicate that this centre is also prepared for the testing of long-range missiles. In addition, it has an assembly shop, a hangar, a test station, six test positions, and tracking and logistical facilities. (3) The Chang Hsin Tien missile testing ground, which has facilities for engine testing.[46]

As far as missile personnel are concerned, Communist China has also established training institutes such as the Science and Technology University in the Chinese Academy of Science, the Tsinghua University, the Peking Aeronautical Engineering College, the Institute of Upper Atmosphere Physics (in Wuhan), the Institute of Automation and Remote Control (in Peking), and the Institute of Mechanics and Electronics (in Peking). Communist China also has many prominent senior experts on missiles and rockets, like Chieng Hsueh-shen (or Tsien Hsue-shen) and Chien Wei-chang. Chieng has played a leading role in Communist China's missile tests.[47]

FUTURE PROSPECT

In view of its present rate of nuclear weapons development, Communist China will very probably become a major nuclear power in the foreseeable future. As early as 1965 United States Defence Secretary McNamara had predicted that Communist China would produce enough fissionable material to start small stockpiles by 1967.[48] In October 1966 Dr R. E. Lapp observed that Communist China could have one hundred atomic bombs and missile warheads by 1967.[49] This was confirmed by Japanese military officials later in 1967,[50] who estimated that Communist China already had about one hundred nuclear bombs. In June 1967 another report conservatively estimated that Communist China already had at least thirty bombs.[51]

Discussing Communist China's delivery capability after its first nuclear test in 1964, Professor R. Hilsman warned that it could be capable of delivering weapons within five to ten years instead of ten to twelve years as United States officials estimated.[52] In early 1966 McNamara estimated that Communist China would be able to launch a nuclear attack on countries within 500 miles of her borders within two to three years.[53] The fourth test in October 1966 indicated that both estimates were for the most part correct. Later in the same year H. W. Baldwin observed that Communist China already had some small nuclear warheads that could be delivered over short distances.[54] In 1967 Senator Henry Jackson, a Congressional spokesman, warned that Communist China would shortly deploy missiles that could deliver nuclear weapons on targets within 1000 miles of its borders and would be capable of launching a nuclear attack on the United States by the early 1970s.[55] Less pessimistically, the Senate–House Atomic Energy Committee estimated that Communist China might have a sizeable force of I.R.B.M.s and M.R.B.M.s by 1975–85. In February 1970 Laird pointed out that Communist China could have a stockpile of 80–100 operational M.R.B.M.s by the mid-1970s.[56]

In 1970, the U.S. State Department said that Communist China should have a medium-range ballistic system soon and a moderate intercontinental ballistic missile force by the mid-1970s.[57] J. I. Coffey, chief of the Office of National Security Studies of Bendix System Division, can only say that Communist China would not have a token I.C.B.M. force by 1975.[58] Laird, in his 1970 statement, also pointed out that he believed that Communist China would test her first I.C.B.M. in the near future.[59] In fact, on 24 April 1970, Communist China successfully launched her first space satellite. The satellite weighed 173 kilogrammes and broadcast the music of 'The East is Red' at a frequency of 20.009 megacycles. Another satellite, identical to the first one, was launched in early 1971.[60]

The above discussion indicates that at the present rate Communist China will become a major nuclear power, possibly within the next fifteen years.

5 China's present Nuclear Strategy

CRITICS of Communist China express the opinion that it is an irresponsible and dangerous nuclear power because of its alleged claim that a third world war is inevitable and that it would not matter much if even half of the world population were to die in that war. For example, the Soviet Union claimed that

To prevent a new world war is a real and quite feasible task. The 20th Congress of our party came to the extremely important conclusion that in our times there is no fatal inevitability of war between states. This conclusion is not the fruit of good intentions, but the result of a realistic, strictly scientific analysis of the balance of class forces on the world arena. . . And what is the position of the C.P.C. leadership? What do the theses that they propagate mean: an end cannot be put to wars so long as imperialism exists. . .

These theses mean that the Chinese comrades are acting contrary to the general course of the world communism movement in questions of war and peace. They do not believe in the possibility of preventing a new world war. . .[1]

Ernst Henri, a noted Russian journalist, pointed out that 'Peking has . . . decided that a third world war is inevitable for the realisation of Mao's master plan'.[2] The Soviet Union further accused Communist China of belittling human lives. It claimed that Communist China had said this:

'Can one guess', he [Mao] said, 'how great the toll of human

47

casualties in a future war will be? Possibly it would be a third of the 2700 million inhabitants of the entire world, i.e. only 900 million people. I consider this to be even low, if atomic bombs should actually fall. Of course it is most terrible. But even half would not be so bad. Why? Because it was not we that wanted it but they. It is they who are imposing war on us. If we fight, atomic and hydrogen weapons will be used. Personally, I think that in the whole world there will be such suffering that half of humanity and perhaps more than a half will perish.

'I [Mao] had an argument about this with Nehru. In this respect he is more pessimistic than I am. I told him that if half of humanity is destroyed, the other half will still remain but imperialism will be destroyed entirely and there will be only socialism in all the world, and within half a century, or a whole century, the population will again increase by even more than half.'[3]

Thus, the Soviet Union said, 'every communist Leninist will feel disgust at an attitude to thermonuclear war such as this: 'Never mind if half of mankind perishes, if 300 million Chinese die. . .'[4] What is more, the Soviet Union pointed out that the Chinese Communist statement 'was no chance remark but considered conception'.[5]

All these accusations were denied by Communist China. It claimed that Mao had only said the following:

At present another situation has to be taken into account, namely, that the war maniacs may drop atomic and hydrogen bombs everywhere. They drop them and we act after their fashion; thus there will be chaos and lives will be lost. The question has to be considered for the worst. The Political Bureau of our Party has held several sessions to discuss this question. If fighting breaks out now, China has got only hand-grenades and not atomic bombs – which the Soviet Union has, though. Let us imagine, how many people will die if war should break out? Out of the world's population of 2700 million, one-third – or, if more, half – may be lost. It is they and not we who want to fight; when a fight starts, atomic and hydrogen bombs may be dropped. I debated this question with a foreign statesman [Nehru]. He believed that if an atomic war was fought, the whole of mankind would be annihilated. I said that if the worst came to the worst and half of mankind died, the other half would remain while imperialism would be razed to the ground and the whole world would become socialist; in a number of years there would be 2700 million people again and definitely more.[6]

Communist China asserts that '(1) China wants peace, and not war; (2) it is the imperialists, and not we, who want to fight; (3) a world war can be prevented'.[7]

It seems that although it has advocated revolutionary wars, armed struggle, and the elimination of imperialist countries, Communist China has not claimed that a world war is inevitable. Nor has it sought such a war. Instead, statements like the one quoted above show more apprehension than aggressiveness. 'It is they and not we who want to fight. . .' Communist China's other apparently bellicose statements are of the same nature :

Should the U.S. imperialists invade China's mainland, we will take all necessary measures to defeat them. . . With the defeat of U.S. imperialism, the time will come when imperialism and colonialism will be really liquidated throughout the world.[8]

Another charge against Communist China is that it 'obviously underestimate[s] the whole danger of thermonuclear war' because it has contended that 'the atomic bomb is a paper tiger' and is not terrible at all.[9]

Communist China has through the years advocated the 'paper tiger' assumption. As early as 1938, Mao Tse-tung had said that 'weapons are an important factor in war, but not the decisive factor; it is people, not things, that are decisive'.[10] This assumption was later extended to include nuclear weapons. In 1961, for instance, Communist China maintained :

The army and regular weapons are necessary to terminate war, to destroy the enemy, to occupy positions, and to win a victory. To rely on the army and regular weapons is to rely primarily on man. The final conclusion thus rests on men.[11]

The Chinese attitude remained unchanged after its first nuclear test in 1964.

The atomic bomb is a paper tiger. This famous statement by Chairman Mao Tse-tung is known to all. This was our view in the past and this is still our view at present.[12]

However, the 'men over weapons' or 'paper tiger' arguments do not necessarily mean that Communist China does not understand the implications of nuclear weapons. In fact, as early as 1954, Communist China had warned its people that

with the appearance of the atomic, hydrogen and other types of weapons of mass destruction, a new war will bring greater sacrifices of lives and material power beyond comparison with former wars.[13]

In 1961, Marshal Yeh Chien-ying advised his troops to learn how to preserve their lives in a nuclear attack.[14] Communist China is particularly concerned about its vulnerable industrial and commercial centres, which are concentrated in and limited to certain areas of the Chinese mainland.[15] In February 1964 Chou En-lai claimed that 'the imperialists and certain other persons have unscrupulously distorted China's position and made widespread propaganda about it'. He pointed out that in a nuclear war Communist China would lose more people than would other countries.[16]

Thus, there is little reason to maintain that Communist China does not understand the implications of nuclear weapons. It fully realises that the 'paper tiger' is quite capable of becoming a 'living tiger' or an 'iron tiger'.

However, it is one thing to say that Communist China does not want a world nuclear war, does not belittle the lives of human beings, and does not underestimate the mass destruction caused by nuclear weapons; and it is another to say that it will therefore not pursue its major foreign policy objectives. At present, since Communist China does not yet have an operational force, it probably will not try to change the present system through 'revolutionary wars', which can help it establish its hegemony at least in Asia and hence serve both its ideological and national interests.

It is over these 'revolutionary wars' that the Communist Chinese are in conflict with the Russians. The Soviet Union particularly opposed the Chinese-sponsored 'revolutionary wars' which, as mentioned earlier, resort only to armed force, violence, and 'the barrel of a gun'. The Soviet Union regards such 'revolutionary wars' as highly dangerous because they might lead to a nuclear war. The Soviet Union, therefore, strongly attacks the Chinese-sponsored revolutionary wars :

> Revising the teaching of Marxist–Leninism, revising the general line of the Communist movement, the Chinese leaders are trying to impose on the international working class and the national liberation movement the theory of speeding revolution by means of 'revolutionary wars'.
> They believe that only in this way can the socialist countries advance the cause of the revolution in the capitalist countries.[17]

In the view of the Soviet Union, peaceful transition of power during revolution should be encouraged and recognised. Because non-peaceful methods are not the primary emphasis, the Soviet Union points out, there is no danger of a nuclear war in the Russian-sponsored revolutions.

Communist China, however, finds the Soviet argument unconvincing. Instead, it urges 'the oppressed peoples and nations' not to abandon their revolutions or refrain from waging revolutionary wars because of their fear of nuclear weapons.[18] What is more, Communist China claims that in revolutionary wars, there is no danger of a nuclear war :

> In recent years, certain persons have been spreading the argument that a single spark from a war of national liberation or from a revolutionary people's war will lead to a world conflagration destroying the whole of mankind. What are the facts? . . . Do not the facts demonstrate the absurdity of this argument?[19]

In comparison, it would appear that the Soviet Union is more cautious in this regard than Communist China. Although the Chinese approach to revolutions does not necessarily indicate a Chinese lack of the fear of a nuclear war, it does suggest a dangerous attitude. For instance, if Communist China is really convinced that its 'revolutionary wars' are in no danger of being escalated into a nuclear war, it might on some extreme occasions tend to encourage or support these wars to the very end with its conventional forces, and therefore neglect the danger of mis-calculation and mis-escalation which might readily lead to a nuclear war.

To what extent, however, or how vigorously would Communist China support the revolutionary wars in the world today? The Communist Chinese have often said that in a revolution self-reliance is necessary.

> The people's armed force led by our party independently waged people's war on a large scale and won great victories without any material aid from outside, both during the more than eight years of the anti-Japanese war and during the more than three years of the people's war of liberation.[20]

They also maintain that a revolutionary war is doomed to failure if it relies entirely on foreign aid.

> To make a revolution and to fight a people's war and be victorious, it is imperative to adhere to the policy of self-reliance. . . If one does not operate by one's own efforts . . . and does not rely on the strength of the masses but leans wholly on foreign aid – even though this be aid from socialist countries which persist in revolution – no victory can be won, or be consolidated even if it is won.[21]

But does this mean that Communist China would not actively support the 'revolutionary war'? The answer is no! Communist China in fact has *never* denied the necessity of foreign aid and support in a revolutionary war. In 1935, for instance, Mao Tse-tung said that 'international support is necessary for the revolutionary struggle today in any country or of any nation'.[22] Mao once admitted that it was a mistake to say that revolution was possible without outside aid because

> in the epoch in which imperialism exists, it is impossible for a genuine people's revolution to win victory in any country without various forms of help from the international revolutionary forces.[23]

Thus, Communist China has already provided itself with a perfect rationale for giving support and aid to revolutionary wars in other countries. In fact, Communist China has maintained that its prime concern is to support revolutions :

> There are two attitudes towards the national democratic revolutionary movement. The first is to maintain good relationships with the Western countries, giving no or little support to the national revolutionary movement. The second is to support the national movement as a general principle, with the possibility of having some contacts with the Western countries but only for secondary reasons. Our country adopted the latter attitude, with the firm resolution to support the national democratic revolutionary movement, and oppose colonialism and imperialism.[24]

Communist China also maintains that 'it is a manifestation of the proletarian internationalism of the Chinese Communist Party when it gives full support to the constantly growing national liberation movements in Asia, Africa and Latin America'.[25] To support revolutionary wars, therefore, is a Communist Chinese obligation :

> The C.C.P. [Chinese Communist Party] has always held that the socialist countries should support the people's revolutionary civil wars. To fail to do so would be to renounce their proletarian internationalist duty.[26]

In 1965, China further pointed out that 'those countries which have won victory are in duty bound to support and aid the peoples who have not done so'.[27] Even nuclear weapons should not change the obligation of the socialist countries to support revolutionary wars.[28] Thus, the Soviet Union's reluctance to support these wars has been referred to by Communist China as a 'shameful betrayal of revolutionary Marxist–Leninist principles', and as appeasing the imperialists at the expense of the interests of the revolutionary people.[29]

Regardless of its support and encouragement of these and other revolutionary wars, Communist China is probably not at present willing to contribute a large number of regular troops, on a scale similar to that of the Korean war, or to use its token nuclear weapons to support these wars. In fact, Communist China has denied its direct involvement in these wars. For example, when it was recently asked by the Cambodian government to explain its intention of building the Lao–Yunnan highways in Laos, Communist China flatly denied its involvement with Laos at all, although in fact it had at least 3000 road builders there along with two infantry battalions equipped with anti-aircraft guns to protect the workers.[30] The main reason for the reluctance to give large-scale support might be that Communist China fears that open support with troops, let alone nuclear weapons, might provoke the United States or provide it with an excuse to launch an attack on mainland China or the Chinese nuclear facilities. Evidence indicates that this fear dates from approximately 1954. In that year, Marshal Yeh Chienying warned his people to prepare against a sudden attack by the 'imperialists', and admitted that in a nuclear war China's army would be in a comparatively backward position.[31] In 1964, after its first nuclear test, Communist China openly admitted that American nuclear forces in Asia were a threat to China's security.

> Everybody knows that U.S. imperialism has been applying its nuclear threats to China and has even gone to the extent of placing nuclear weapons at the very doors of China. The U.S. Seventh Fleet, carrying nuclear arms, prowls up and down China's coastal waters. One U.S. nuclear base after another has been built around China. U.S. military and political chiefs have truculently threatened to drop nuclear bombs on China.[32]

Later, Communist China appeared to believe that the United States might be tempted to launch a sudden nuclear attack on China :

> The perfidious imperialists are accustomed to launch sudden attacks in starting an aggressive war, and new techniques create more favourable conditions for carrying out sudden military attacks.[33]

In other statements, Communist China indicates that the United States must take the initiative in waging a war on China :

> The Chinese people are ready to make all necessary sacrifices in the fight against imperialism. *It is up to the U.S. President and the Pentagon to decide whether the United States wants*

a big war with China today. . . If the imperialists are determined to launch a war of aggression against us, they are welcome to come sooner, to come as early as tomorrow. . .
For sixteen years we have been waiting for *the U.S. imperialists to come in and attack us.* My hair has turned grey in waiting. Perhaps I will not have the luck to see the U.S. imperialist invasion of China, but my children may see it, and they will resolutely carry on the fight. Let no correspondent think that I am bellicose. *It is the U.S. imperialists who are brutal and vicious* and who bully others too much. . .*[34]

It appears that Communist China still considers an American attack to be possible. In other words, Communist China might fear that attacking China is still a viable American option, especially under such circumstances as a massive and direct Chinese involvement in the 'revolutionary war'. It seems that this consideration has at least partially contributed to the containment of Communist China in the past years.

* My italics.

6 China as an Operational Nuclear Power and its Nuclear Strategy

WHEN Communist China becomes an operational nuclear power, with a small stockpile of M.R.B.M.s or I.R.B.M.s, a new type of nuclear deterrence, between Communist China on the one hand and one or both of the superpowers on the other, will emerge. So far both superpowers have been able to maintain a relatively stable international system. The United States, for example, has played a significant role in the maintenance of world security and stability, especially in Asia. Thus in 1964, immediately after Communist China had conducted its first nuclear test, President Johnson assured American allies in Asia that the American commitments there would be honoured, and announced at the same time that 'nations that do not seek nuclear weapons can be sure that if they need United States support against the threat of nuclear blackmail, they will have it'.[1] Since 1960, the Soviet Union has refused to support or encourage Chinese nuclear development. In fact the Russian attitude has changed over the past years from apparent indifference to indirect attack and then to open attack of Communist China's nuclear development.[2]

However, it is questionable whether the present deterrence will remain effective once Communist China possesses an operational nuclear force. In that event, it is doubtful whether the United States would be willing to continue to honour its present commitments in Asia. Johnson's guarantee was not mentioned after

57

1964. In fact, on 19 July 1967, one month after the sixth Chinese test was conducted, American Secretary of State Dean Rusk announced that the guarantees mentioned by Johnson in 1964 would only be discussed again in Geneva, where the Nuclear Non-proliferation Treaty would be negotiated, or in the Security Council of the United Nationals.[3] On 26 April 1968 Arthur J. Goldberg, United States ambassador to the General Assembly, stated that

> in the view of the United States, aggression with nuclear weapons or the threat of such aggression against a non-nuclear state would create a qualitative new situation – a situation in which the nuclear-weapon states which are permanent members of the United Nations Security Council would have to act immediately through the Security Council to take measures necessary to counter such aggression or to remove the threat of aggression in accordance with the United Nations Charter.[4]

It appears that the United States has gradually reduced its commitments to defend, by itself, the security of Asian countries against a possible Chinese nuclear threat. Instead, it would prefer to see an international body assume the responsibility.

The United States is by no means the only country proposing such a U.N. guarantee. The ideal of a 'multilateral assurance through the United Nations' has long been sponsored by others. In 1966, for example, Frank Aiken, the Irish Foreign Minister, said :

> I have already indicated my conviction that armed resistance to aggression by individual states or by limited group alliance is ceasing to give them the assurance of permanent security against attack by a great nuclear power. This assurance, in my opinion, can only be given in the nuclear missile age with the maximum of credibility by a world-wide system of collective security based on a United Nations peace-guarantor force composed of lightly armed troops drawn from the non-nuclear Members, and backed by a combined force supplied by the nuclear powers who have bound themselves to oppose aggression by a nuclear power on a non-nuclear State.[5]

This U.N. guarantee, if possible and effective, is of course desirable. Unfortunately, however, it does not seem to be very likely. Because of the impotence of the United Nations' own collective security system, the ineffectiveness of the Security Council because of the use of veto power, and the other organisational weaknesses and political problems in the United Nations, an effective U.N. guarantee is beyond present attainment. The United Nations has yet to make any visible progress in this direction.

However, a joint U.S.–Soviet guarantee for the security of Asian countries has been proposed.[6] The alleged significance of this 'joint guarantee' is that it would not juxtapose the great powers. This joint guarantee seems feasible to Raymond Aron, because he believes that 'the big powers will act jointly to restrain potential troublemakers, even those armed with nuclear weapons'.[7] Furthermore, to realise such a joint guarantee, the superpowers do not need overall co-operation. However, such optimism seems unwarranted. True, in recent years there has been some limited co-operation between the superpowers, e.g. their joint efforts in the neutralisation of Laos, in the mediation of the Indian–Pakistan war of 1965 and the later Tashkent agreement, their meetings in Glassboro and Camp David, and their common effort in the Partial Nuclear Test Ban Treaty and the Nuclear Non-proliferation Treaty. Nevertheless, the scope of their co-operation is still limited. Basic conflicts of interest between the superpowers are still quite real. It is therefore extremely unlikely that the Soviet Union would agree to a joint guarantee of the security of South Vietnam; nor is it likely that the United States would agree to a guarantee with the Russians of the security of North Vietnam. In this regard, Stanley Hoffmann seems correct when he points out :

> As long as the bipolar contest persists, one may doubt the willingness of each superpower to give an assurance to non-nuclear allies or clients of the other, against a former or dissident ally, and thus to consecrate formally the fiasco of the original alliance, and perhaps even to consolidate the rival's hold on an area.[8]

Thus, it is very doubtful whether a 'joint guarantee' would be a feasible solution to the problem of security in Asia.

Even if such a guarantee for security were offered by the superpowers, it would still be doubtful whether it would be effective in deterring a possible Chinese nuclear attack.

Unless the guarantees have a terrifying degree of automaticity and certainty – i.e. promise of nuclear retaliation against the state that uses nuclear weapons first on an adversary – they may have little deterrent effect on a state that may hope to knock out its foe in a single blow, and then turn to the guarantors and point out to them the vanity of further bloodshed, or plead that it was provoked.[9]

Thus, the credibility of such a guarantee, if it were at all possible, would still present a serious problem. The Asian countries might doubt that the United States or the Soviet Union could stop or deter a Chinese nuclear attack in time to save their countries from destruction. It would certainly be useless to rescue a ruined land. Furthermore, some Asians believe that Communist China tends to take military action against its enemies when both superpowers are occupied by other crises in the world. They believe, for instance, that Communist China decided to attack India in October 1962 because it calculated that while the superpowers were engaged in the Cuban crisis, they would not be able to intervene in Asian affairs.[10] Therefore, even presuming that there was a guarantee, the superpowers still might not be able to honour it.

Therefore, the only way to 'guarantee' security would be 'an American presence, complete with missiles and/or planes', which 'would undoubtedly have a very salutary effect, particularly in psychological terms, on the credibility problem'.[11] But then, such a 'trip wire' situation[12] would be extremely dangerous because a Chinese attack on a guaranteed country would be tantamount to attacking the United States. Consequently it would be physically impossible for the United States to avoid involvement in a war with Communist China. It is very doubtful whether either superpower would be willing to risk putting itself in such a situation.

In addition, the United States will be in an uncomfortable position when Communist China has an operational nuclear force and is in a position to attack many of the American bases in Asia. If Communist China were to attack a country whose security was guaranteed by the United States, the Americans would have to take into consideration the possibility that retaliation on their part might provoke a Communist Chinese nuclear attack on U.S. bases in Asia, and hence ignite a Sino–American nuclear war or possibly a world nuclear war. The United States would certainly not be willing to accept the consequences of such a war.

Thus, when Communist China becomes an operational nuclear power, the effectiveness of the nuclear deterrence imposed by the superpowers in Asia would significantly diminish. The situation in Asia might become even more unstable if the United States no longer considered it expedient to keep its military commitments in Asia, particularly in South and South-East Asia. Consequently, it might decide to withdraw from this area, rather than confront a nuclear China.

Furthermore, as the Chinese nuclear capability grows, Communist China itself appears to feel that the superpowers' nuclear deterrence is becoming less effective.[13] Thus an announcement was made following each Chinese nuclear test, claiming that it was a further encouragement of revolutionary wars. In 1964, for instance, after its first nuclear test, China declared:

The mastering of the nuclear weapons by China is a great encouragement to the revolutionary peoples of the world in their struggles.[14]

A few days after the test, China's official organ, *People's Daily*, carried an editorial which stated:

The fifteen-year history of New China proves that in the struggle against the imperialist policies of aggression and war, for supporting the revolutionary movements of all peoples and safeguarding world peace, socialist China can be fully trusted.[15]

A similar statement was made by China after its third nuclear test[16] on 9 May 1966:

The Chinese people's possession of nuclear weapons is a great encouragement to the peoples who are fighting heroically for their own liberation. . .[17]

It is very significant to note that before its fourth nuclear test, a guided missile–nuclear weapon test, China had never in its nuclear test statements specifically encouraged any particular revolutionary war such as that in Vietnam. Instead, it only vaguely claimed that China's nuclear weapons development was a great encouragement to the revolutionary peoples of the world. Such an omission indicates the caution with which China described the military and political significance of its first nuclear weapons achievements. At least it indicates that China did not want to antagonise the United States and other non-Communist countries in Asia by pointing out any particular revolution it encouraged. This assumption is supported by many writers. For example, Alice L. Hsieh pointed out :

> According to Peking's propaganda, the mastering of nuclear weapons technology through China's own efforts was a great encouragement to the revolutionary peoples of the world. . . The Chinese, however, carefully avoided any specific application of this principle to concrete situations, such as those in Vietnam and Laos.[18]

Similarly, John W. Finney in an article in the *New York Times* pointed out :

> Through the Peking statements have run the theme that the atomic tests represent a key step in China's progress toward great-power status and an increase in China's national defense capability. But the statements were . . . cautious in assessing the military implications of the tests.
>
> For example, Peking has emphasised that China's mastering of nuclear weapons technology is a great encouragement to the revolutionary peoples of the world. The Chinese leaders, however, avoided any specific application of this principle to concrete situations, such as in Vietnam or Laos. . .[19]

On this assumption, China's estimate of the significance of its nuclear weapons capability has certainly increased since its fourth nuclear test. On 27 October 1966, after its guided missile–nuclear test, China claimed :

> The possession by the Chinese people of guided missiles and

nuclear weapons is a great encouragement to the heroic Vietnamese people who are waging a war of resistance against U.S. aggression and for national salvation, and to all the revolutionary peoples of the world who are now engaged in heroic struggles. . .[20]

Thus 'a specific application', i.e. the encouragement of a particular revolution, was presented. A similar statement was made by China after its fifth nuclear test.[21]

In June 1967, after its sixth nuclear test, China began to add the Arab people to those whom its claimed to have been encouraged and supported by China's nuclear weapons achievement:

It is a very great encouragement and support to the Vietnamese people in their heroic war against United States aggression and for national salvation, to the Arab people in their resistance to aggression by the United States and British imperialists and their tool, Israel, and to the revolutionary peoples of the whole world.[22]

In December 1968, after conducting its eighth nuclear test, China made a similar statement.[23]

After successfully conducting two more nuclear tests in October 1969, China identified more particular revolutions that it claimed were both supported and encouraged by its nuclear weapons achievement.

These new achievements in China's development of nuclear weapons . . . are a great encouragement and support to the heroic Vietnamese people who are courageously carrying on the war against U.S. aggression and for national salvation, to Laotian people who are fighting against the armed invasion by U.S. imperialism and the reactionaries of Thailand, to the Palestinian and other Arab people who are resisting the U.S. imperialist Zionist aggression, and to the people of all countries who are fighting for people's liberation.[24]

Therefore, it appears that as China's nuclear weapons capability grows, China has also changed its attitude towards the impact of its nuclear tests on revolutionary wars. The original vague and cautious statement that its nuclear weapons achievement was 'a great encouragement to the revolutionary peoples' has been replaced by the more specific and concrete statement that it encourages the Vietnamese, the Laotian and other revolutionary wars. The 'enemies' were also clearly identified, namely the United States, Thailand, etc.

The above analysis indicates that Communist China feels that, as its nuclear weapons capability increases, a new type of deterrence, more to its advantage than the previous type, is being developed, especially in Asia. Therefore, pro-Chinese revolutionary elements might be put in a position where they could initiate revolutionary wars without being troubled by the threat of hostile intervention, even on the part of the United States. Thus revolutionary activity in Asia might be substantially increased. Communist China might also intensify its military and material aid to these revolutionary elements. Already, North Vietnam has claimed that the Chinese nuclear tests were a great encouragement to its struggle against U.S. aggression.[25] The Laotian Patriotic Front claimed that the Chinese tests had been a powerful inspiration to its cause of fighting the United States. The Communist Party of Malaya described the tests as a 'tremendous encouragement and a powerful support to struggle for national liberation'. The Communist Party of Thailand declared that they were an immense encouragement to the people of Thailand, who are struggling against imperialism. Similarly the Ceylonese Communist Party regarded the tests as an encouragement and 'support' to all 'oppressed peoples' struggling for their liberation.[26] Many anti-Communist countries fear that the Chinese nuclear weapons development might encourage revolutionary wars in Asia. For example, Thai Premier Thanon and Malayan Deputy Premier Razak both stated that the tests would encourage other Communist subversive activities.[27]

At the same time, Communist China's nuclear weapons development has also caused fear among other Asian countries. For example, P. K. Banerjee, Minister of the Indian Embassy in Washington, said that Communist China's nuclear test had brought a 'sense of insecurity and offensive threat, not only to India but to many neighbouring countries'.[28] The Indian Prime Minister, Shastri, pointed out that it was necessary to have some guarantee from the superpowers for the security of India.[29] A

Ceylonese newspaper asked, 'has the performance of the Chinese lately in crossing the Himalayan passes already become a dim memory?'[30] Japanese Prime Minister Sato said that the Communist Chinese nuclear test increased the importance of a nuclear guarantee for the security of other Asian countries.[31] 'China with a nuclear capability is, as far as Japan is concerned, a threat.'[32] Cambodia expressed its fear in its recurrent statements reminding Communist China that it 'has solemnly declared that it will never be the first to use these weapons of mass destruction'.[33]

The Asian countries' fear of a nuclear China might have the following consequences. First, these countries might become reluctant to resist Chinese-sponsored revolutionary wars in their own countries. Secondly, they might consider it expedient to join in the Chinese hegemony and follow the Chinese line of policy. Thirdly, they might accede to Chinese demands without resistance in incidents such as border disputes. As Sisir Gupta points out :

> China may subject a non-nuclear India to periodic blackmail, weaken its people's spirit of resistance and self-confidence and thus achieve without a war its major political objectives in Asia. India's experience with China suggests that such a course of action is not only possible but probable.[34]

Thus, when Communist China becomes an operational nuclear power, its blackmail policy might become effective in Asia.

With an operational nuclear force, Communist China might also attempt limited military actions in Asia, similar to the occupation of Aksai Chin at the time of the Sino–Indian war. If the war in Vietnam continues to such a time or if new fighting were to start in Korea, Communist China might even send its 'voluntary' troops into these areas. It might also send regular troops across its borders into countries like Thailand and Burma, either openly to support revolutionary wars or to occupy territory. It might also launch a conventional attack on Quemoy or Taiwan to eliminate the Nationalist Chinese, an action it has vowed to take ever since 1949.

Through nuclear blackmail, Communist China might also try to force Asian countries to remove United States bases from their territories. The removal of United States bases from Asia has been one of Communist China's objectives since 1949. Before its first nuclear test, however, Communist China had employed an 'Asian nuclear-free zone' strategy. At that time it advocated the establishment of a 'nuclear-weapon-free zone of the Asian and Pacific region' in which all countries would be required to

> dismantle all military bases, including nuclear bases, on foreign soil, and withdraw from abroad all nuclear weapons and their means of delivery . . . [and to] establish a nuclear-weapon-free zone of the Asian and Pacific region, including the United States, the Soviet Union, China and Japan. . .[35]

Once this 'zone' was established, the superpowers' nuclear forces would be withdrawn from Asia, and their deterrent effect on Communist China would be significantly reduced.

Apparently, Communist China decided to change its strategy after its 1964 nuclear test. It probably judged that the establishment of a 'nuclear-free zone' in Asia would also prohibit its own nuclear tests. Thus on 22 November 1964 Communist China began to question the usefulness of this zone, which it had previously supported:

> Many countries at present are keenly interested in the establishment of nuclear-free zones. However, to really free the nuclear-free zones from the threats of nuclear war it is first necessary for the nuclear powers to undertake not to use nuclear weapons. Otherwise, the establishment of nuclear-free zones would be impossible and even if they be set up in name, all it means is that the non-nuclear countries would be deprived of their legitimate right to develop nuclear weapons to resist the nuclear menace and be bound hand and foot.[36]

The purpose of this new strategy is obvious. If such a pledge was made by the superpowers, their nuclear deterrence on China would be greatly reduced, even if there was not a 'nuclear-free zone' in Asia. However, since Communist China appears to realise that the superpowers would not give such a pledge, it has used another strategy to remove United States bases from Asia. On 24 November 1964, for instance, after Japanese Prime Minister Sato decided to permit United States nuclear submarines in Japanese ports, Communist China warned:

The closer the Japan–U.S. collaboration, the less guaranteed is Japan's security. Today U.S. imperialism is brandishing its nuclear weapons in Asia, making active preparations for a nuclear war. If it eventually starts such a war, Japan, as a U.S. nuclear base, is bound to bear the brunt and will inevitably be pushed into the abyss of nuclear calamity. The Japanese Government willingly acts as an accomplice in U.S. imperialism's nuclear war preparations – this is an extremely dangerous road by which the Japanese nation is led to a bottomless nuclear chasm. Precisely because of this, the Japanese people have unfolded a vigorous mass struggle opposing entry of U.S. nuclear submarines and opposing turning Japan into a U.S. nuclear war base by the U.S.–Japanese reactionaries.[37]

Communist China might also use potential threats to prevent Asian countries from becoming allies of either superpower. At present, although Communist China has only a token nuclear capability, it has already tended to use this strategy towards Japan :

Placing itself [Japan] under the wing of U.S. imperialism, working hand in glove with Soviet revisionism . . . and acting as the vanguard in opposing China, the reactionary Sato government will . . . end shamelessly in being buried together with U.S. imperialism and Soviet revisionism.[38]

If the United States indeed decided to remove its bases from Asia, or even to withdraw its commitment from Asia, the deterrence it has imposed on Communist China would be further eroded. As mentioned earlier, without the presence of U.S. force in Asia the credibility of American guarantees – if there still are any – over Asian countries' security would be seriously reduced. Furthermore, it might be too late for the United States to save a victim of a Chinese nuclear attack. Thus, behind its nuclear umbrella, Communist China's huge ground force could become a very effective instrument in the pursuit of its foreign policy objectives. At present, Communist China has an army of 2,500,000 men in 115 divisions. It also has four armoured divisions and one or two airborne divisions. In addition, it has a militia of 250 million men and women, well trained for ground combat, guerrilla warfare, close combat and night fighting.[39] Therefore, they would be most effective in Thailand, Malaysia, Laos, Vietnam and Burma, where jungles, cliffs and swamps make the terrain suitable for guerrilla warfare. The highways mentioned previously would make transportation of supplies and troops easier than it has been in the past.[40] In addition, there is evidence that Communist China is prepared to equip its ground troops with tactical nuclear weapons and may well be considering their use on the battlefield.[41]

It may be suggested that Asian countries could still unite in order to halt any possible future Communist Chinese aggression or Chinese-sponsored revolutionary wars in Asia.[42] The possibility of this collective 'defence', unfortunately, appears to be rather small. In the first place, there are various conflicts and tensions among countries in Asia, e.g. between Pakistan and India, among Indonesia–Malaysia–the Philippines, between Malaysia and Singapore, and among Cambodia, Thailand and Vietnam. In the second place, the foreign policies of these countries are entirely different, ranging from completely anti-Communist (Nationalist China, South Vietnam, South Korea) to pro-Communist Chinese 'non-aligned' (Burma, Nepal, Pakistan and, the Neutralist Lao). In the third place, most Asian countries are incapable of defending themselves without outside assistance. The combination of weaknesses among these countries does not necessarily mean strength. Only India, Indonesia and Japan are strong in relation to Communist China. But both India and Indonesia have been plagued by many domestic and foreign problems and have been weakened in recent years. As far as Japan is concerned, most Asian countries probably still remember vividly the Japanese invasion and aggression in Asia during the Second World War. Their fear of a strong Japan might therefore rule out any possibility of supporting Japan as their leader in Asia against Communist China.

Writers such as Alastair Buchan then suggest that the Asian countries could arm themselves with nuclear weapons to balance the nuclear capability of Communist China.[43] At present, there are two countries in Asia which might employ this alternative: Japan and India.

India has long been a country opposed to a domestic nuclear weapons programme. In 1961 Prime Minister Nehru announced that under no circumstances would India develop nuclear weapons.[44] However, by 1965, there seemed to be a change of Indian position in this regard. Prime Minister Shastri said at the Indian National Congress of that year that 'I do not know what may happen later, but our present policy is not to build an atom bomb, and it is the right policy'.[45] Apparently, India's position was no longer as rigid as it had been. Then, in September 1968, after Communist China had conducted its seventh test, the Indian Defence Studies and Analysis Institute urged the Indian government to build up the necessary facilities for future nuclear weapons development.[46] Some experts, such as Leonard Beaton, even said that India might already have begun the design of a plutonium bomb.[47] A report in January 1970 says that there are persistent demands from within India's ruling Congress Party for an Indian nuclear weapon programme and that the Indian government is now studying the cost of building such a system.[48]

As far as Japan is concerned, it particularly wishes not to fall too far behind Communist China in nuclear weapons development.[49] Therefore, although Japan is a party to the Nuclear Non-proliferation Treaty, a nuclear weapons programme will probably remain a serious alternative for Japan. Furthermore, Japan is technologically capable of developing such weapons. In 1969, to the surprise of the United States Atomic Energy Commission, the Japanese Science and Technology Agency announced that Japanese scientists had developed new techniques for the production of enriched uranium.[50] In 1970 the finance minister of Japan announced that Japan's defence spending will take its sharpest rise since the Second World War. Premier Eisaku Sato also claimed that the possession of nuclear weapons would not violate the anti-military spirit of the Japanese constitution, and that Japan must take greater responsibility for its defence.[51] It appears that Joseph Alsop of the *Los Angeles Times* Service is correct when he said that 'Japan will embark on an independent course and soon thereafter take the necessary steps to become a nuclear power'.[52]

Thus, both India and Japan will become nuclear powers when Communist China possesses an operational nuclear force. When this happens, there will be even less guarantee of stability and security in Asia. In the first place, if Communist China, India and Japan become operational nuclear powers, there might be a rapid nuclear proliferation in Asia or even in the world. If Buchan was correct when he said that 'the biggest gap in the chain reaction of proliferation may be from the fifth to the sixth nuclear powers', proliferation would become inevitable.[53] He also pointed out that as a result of the Chinese nuclear weapons development, many Asian countries might seek to become nuclear countries themselves. Once this takes place, 'there could be no assurance that it would not spread to the Middle East and to Europe'.[54] United States Secretary of Defence McNamara has also said :

> I want to emphasise the dangers of nuclear spread that were dramatised by the detonation at Lop Nor [the Chinese test site]. Nuclear technology is advancing so rapidly that the cost of building a minimum nuclear capability, cost whether measured in terms of capital expenditure, human skills or the time required to achieve that capability, is decreasing dramatically. Nuclear spread, therefore, is one of the greatest dangers facing the world today.[55]

McNamara's warning is by no means unrealistic. At present, in Asia, many countries which are very sensitive to the Chinese, Indian or Japanese nuclear weapons developments, such as Pakistan, Indonesia, South Korea, the Philippines, Thailand, South Vietnam, Nationalist China and Australia, all possess power reactors and have started advanced nuclear research.[56] Either out of fear or pride, or both, they might well decide to develop their own nuclear weapons when Communist China, Japan and India become operational nuclear powers. Further nuclear proliferation would then become inevitable. In the second place, there are many tense local conflicts and potential conflicts in Asia : between Pakistan and India, between North Vietnam and South Vietnam, and between Cambodia and Vietnam or Thailand. There are also potential dangers and conflicts among Malaysia, the Philippines, and Indonesia.

If these countries were to become nuclear countries and hence become more confident of their strength and capability, settlement of their conflicts might become more difficult. Since none of them could expect to have invulnerability or near invulnerability such as the superpowers have, one country might be tempted to launch a pre-emptive nuclear attack on its enemies in order to eliminate them once and for all or to destroy their nuclear facilities before they could become too powerful to deal with. As Herman Kahn points out :

> An irresponsible, desperate, or determined decision maker might not waste time on the lower rungs of the escalation ladder. He might simply launch a disarming attack on his victim and present the world with a *fait accompli.* Even if the potential victim has a nuclear capability, it may not have enough second-strike capability to deter such an attack.[57]

Similar temptation might also exist between Communist China and many Asian countries. For example, if a very hostile India or Thailand were becoming an operational nuclear power, Communist China might be tempted to launch a nuclear attack on the country before it could become a nuclear threat to China.

When Communist China becomes an operational or major nuclear power, the superpowers' self-restraints in the nuclear arms race might also be seriously affected. As mentioned ealier, both superpowers have watched each other's nuclear capability very closely. Thus in 1966, when there were signs that the Soviet Union was developing an effective A.B.M. (Anti-Ballistic Missile), the United States immediately accelerated its nuclear weapons programme to ensure its own 'penetration capability'.[58] The superpowers therefore have maintained a very delicate balance of nuclear capability between themselves. However, neither superpower has been willing to risk an unlimited arms race by wholeheartedly attempting to develop an invulnerable nuclear force.

However, after Communist China successfully tested a nuclear–missile combination and its hydrogen bomb, many Americans started to fear a potential Chinese nuclear threat. For example, Senator Henry Jackson, a Congressional spokesman on U.S. defence, feared that Communist China might be able to launch a nuclear attack on the United States earlier than expected.[59] After the Chinese sixth test on 17 June 1967 many

senior U.S. military analysts began to feel the need for an
A.B.M. system.[60] In the same year, Secretary of Defence
McNamara announced that the United States had decided to
deploy a 'limited anti-ballistic-missile system' against a possible
I.C.B.M. threat from Communist China.[61] He particularly
pointed out that 'the development will foreclose any possibility
of a successful Chinese nuclear attack on the United States and
will thereby provide assurance of our determination to support
our Asian friends against Chinese nuclear blackmail'.[62] On 6
August 1969 the United States officially decided to develop its
A.B.M. programme. One of the main reasons given by President
Nixon for this decision was the 'defence of the American people
against the kind of nuclear attack which Communist China is
likely to be able to mount within the decade'.[63]

Nevertheless, the question remains: how long can this
'limited' or 'thin' A.B.M. system remain effective? In view of
the rapid nuclear development in Communist China, a 'limited'
A.B.M. system might become ineffective before long. In order
to keep up with Chinese nuclear development, the United States
will have constantly to increase the strength of its A.B.M. system.
Eventually, the system would become a 'thick' one. If the Soviet
Union wants to maintain the balance of nuclear capability, as it
certainly would, it too would have to develop a 'thick' A.B.M.
system. Consequently, a rapid arms race might take place between the superpowers. But as a group of prominent scholars,
including Hans J. Morgenthau, Arthur Larson and Edmund A.
Gullison, have pointed out, a further anti-ballistic development
could trigger a costly and potentially suicidal arms race with the
Soviet Union.[64]

The situation might be aggravated by the fact that Communist China is regarded as a potential enemy by both superpowers. Thus when Communist China possesses an operational
nuclear force, either superpower might be tempted to increase
its own nuclear capability to the degree that the nuclear force
of Communist China and of the other superpower would be
matched and therefore deterred. Consequently, a rapid nuclear
arms race among the United States, the Soviet Union and Communist China would become inevitable.

7 Conclusion: China as a Major Nuclear Power and its Effects on the International Political System

IN the near future, Communist China will become a major nuclear power, with a stockpile of I.C.B.M.s and a certain degree of invulnerability of its nuclear force. As a result, there will be three major national actors, namely the United States, the Soviet Union and Communist China, in the international system. Of course, the simple fact that a third major national actor will be added to the international system does not necessarily mean that there will be drastic major change in the structure as well as in the characteristics of the system. However, in the event of Communist China becoming the third major national actor, because of its foreign policy objectives and its relations with other national actors in the system the international system will face many serious stresses.

1. A MILITANT THIRD FORCE

While both superpowers are 'conservative' and 'defensive' in the sense that they both intend to maintain the *status quo* of the international system, Communist China is 'revolutionary' and

73

'offensive' in the sense that it is determined to change the structure and the distribution of powers in the international system.
Thus, when Communist China becomes a major nuclear power,
unless there is a drastic change[1] in Chinese foreign policy objectives it is very likely that it would pursue these objectives more
directly and aggressively. For example, it might use its conventional force directly or use nuclear blackmail to force or induce
many national actors to support China as the leader of a new
power centre in the international system. Communist China
might first try to establish its hegemony among countries in the
traditional political Areas i, ii and iii, which coincide with the
Asian part of the 'first intermediate zone', including countries in
South-East Asia. Afterwards, Communist China might try to
establish its influence through revolutionary wars or subversions
in the rest of the 'first intermediate zone', which coincides with
part of the traditional political Area iv, covering countries in
Africa and Latin America. Verbal hostility towards the 'imperialist countries' and countries in the 'second intermediate zone'
might be transformed into military actions, although a direct and
deliberate attack on the homelands of the superpowers without
provocation would probably not be viable, by Chinese calculations.

It is true that there appears to be a gap between Communist
China's words and deeds, since Chinese bellicose statements have
not been paralleled by actions, which are relatively cautious.
This, however, by no means indicates that Communist China has
put aside its foreign policy objectives.

To understand this peculiar phenomenon, it is first necessary
to understand the difference between 'strategy' and 'tactics' in
Communist Chinese terminology. According to the Chinese
Communists, strategy refers to a war situation as a whole, while
tactics refers to specific instances in a war situation.[2] Although
strategically one has to 'despise' the enemy, tactically one has to
'respect' him :

In fighting imperialism, we are of the opinion that, strategically and with regard to the whole, one must despise the enemy,
dare to struggle against him and dare to seize victory; at the
same time, tactically and with regard to each specific struggle,

one must take the enemy seriously and be prudent. If one does not take full account of the enemy tactically and is heedless and reckless, while strategically one dares not despise the enemy, it is inevitable that one will commit the error of adventurism in tactics and that of capitulationism in strategy.[3]

This attitude did not change after the 1964 nuclear test. In 1965 Communist China said:

Comrade Mao Tse-tung points out that we must despise the enemy strategically and take full account of him tactically.[4]

For this reason, Communist China always 'despises' the enemy in its statements, but remains very cautious in practical situations. To 'respect' the enemy only means to be 'cautious' and 'realistic': this Communist China indeed has been. It by no means indicates, however, that Communist China would de-emphasise its foreign policy objectives; these should still be pursued in earnest. In fact, Communist China insists that a tactical offensive is absolutely necessary.

It is possible and necessary to use tactical offensives within the strategic defensive; to fight campaigns and battles of quick decision within a strategically protracted war and to fight campaigns and battles on exterior lines within strategically interior lines.[5]

At the same time, the meaning of 'strategic defensive' must not be misunderstood either. A 'strategic defensive' is by no means passive or conservative in nature. Instead, its approach is still 'offensive' because 'passive defence' is absolutely unacceptable. As Mao said:

As far as I know, there is no military manual of value nor any sensible military expert, ancient or modern, Chinese or foreign, that does not oppose passive defence, whether in strategy or tactics. Only a complete fool or a madman would cherish passive defence as a talisman. However, there are people in this world who do such things. That is an error in war, a manifestation of conservatism in military matters, which we must resolutely oppose.[6]

Thus, when it becomes a major nuclear power with sufficient strength to act more directly and militantly, Communist China could adopt both tactical and strategic offensive policies in order to achieve its objectives. Its words would then be paralleled by actions. Communist China's attitude towards the Russian I.C.B.M. and satellite successes in 1957 supports this view. In 1957, when the Soviet Union successfully launched its first I.C.B.M. and Sputnik ɪ, Communist China, then the closest ally of the Soviet Union, contended that a fundamental change in the world balance had taken place. Mao said:

It is my opinion that the international situation has now reached a new turning point. There are two winds in the world today, the East wind and the West wind. There is a Chinese saying, 'Either the East wind prevails over the West wind or the West wind prevails over the East wind'. It is characteristic of the situation today, I believe, that the East wind is prevailing over the West wind. That is to say, the forces of socialism are overwhelmingly superior to the forces of imperialism.[7]

On 10 February 1958 Chou En-lai declared that there was a 'new change in the long-standing superiority of the forces of socialism over those of imperialism' and called this 'a new turning-point in the world situation'.[8] For this reason, Communist China urged the Soviet Union to take a more aggressive stand against the United States and its allies. In the same year, Communist China initiated a heavy bombardment of the offshore island of Quemoy, expecting Russian support for further military activities. However, the Soviet Union apparently did not agree with the 'turning-point' theory and told Communist China that it would neither support the Chinese action nor initiate any military ventures in the world. This Soviet attitude forced Communist China, although very unwillingly, to withdraw from further military activities.[9]

Communist China's 1957 'turning-point' theory and 'East over West' argument suggest that when it becomes a major nuclear power it might consider that another 'turning-point' had come and might therefore adopt a more aggressive policy. In fact, developments after 1964 confirm this tendency – the Communist Chinese attitude toward the political and military significance of its nuclear weapons has changed as rapidly as its nuclear weapons development has grown.

Before its first nuclear test in 1964, for instance, China had never indicated that it intended to break the monopoly of nuclear weapons by the superpowers, i.e. the United States and the Soviet Union. China attacked their monopoly of nuclear weapons only indirectly by criticising the Partial Test Ban Treaty they had just signed :

> This is a treaty signed by three nuclear powers. By this treaty they attempt to consolidate their nuclear monopoly and bind the hands of all peace-loving countries subjected to nuclear threat.[10]

However, after its first nuclear test in 1964, China began to argue that its decision to develop nuclear weapons was made in order to break the monopoly of nuclear weapons by the super-powers and that its nuclear test was intended to 'oppose the U.S. imperialist policy of nuclear blackmail and nuclear threat . . . [and] to break the nuclear monopoly of the nuclear powers'.[11] China also claimed that the test was conducted to ensure that the U.S. blackmail and nuclear threat would 'no longer be so effective'.[12] But China, in these and other statements, never claimed that its nuclear test had any direct effects on the superpowers' nuclear monopoly. A similar statement was made by China after its second nuclear test in 1965.[13]

Initially, after it conducted its first hydrogen bomb test in May 1966, China claimed that the purpose of its nuclear weapons development was merely 'to oppose the nuclear black-mail and threats of U.S. imperialism and its collaborators and to oppose the U.S.–Soviet collusion for maintaining nuclear monopoly'.[14] However, apparently believing that it had reached a 'high level of science and technology', thanks to the development of a hydrogen bomb, China began to imply, although very indirectly, that its test was a 'positive factor supporting all people opposing the nuclear monopoly, nuclear threats and joint schemes of the U.S. imperialists and the Khrushchevian revisionists'.[15]

After its fourth test, China repeated that the purpose of its nuclear weapons development was precisely to 'undermine the nuclear monopoly and oppose nuclear blackmail by the super-powers'.[16] But a few days later, on 3 November 1966, China issued another statement in which the word 'blow' was intro-duced to describe the effects of its nuclear weapons achievement on the monopoly of nuclear weapons by the superpowers.[17] Nevertheless, the word 'blow' was not applied directly to the nuclear monopoly by the superpowers. Rather, China merely claimed that the test was a blow to their 'scheme' to perpetuate nuclear monopoly by seeking the Nuclear Non-proliferation Treaty.[18] A similar statement was made by China after its fifth test; but this time, the phrase 'heavy blow' instead of 'blow' was used :

> The success of the three nuclear tests conducted by China in the one year of 1966 is a heavy blow to the plot of U.S. imperialism and Soviet modern revisionism which have been collaborating in a vain attempt to enforce their nuclear monopoly. . .[19]

Up to that moment, China had merely claimed that its tests had only affected the superpowers' 'scheme' or 'plot' of nuclear monopoly and those only in an indirect manner. It declined to make any claims about the direct effects that its nuclear tests might have had on the actual 'nuclear monopoly' of the super-powers.

However, after its sixth nuclear test, China claimed that its nuclear weapons development had further broken the nuclear monopoly of the superpowers :

> China has got atom bombs and guided missiles, and she now has the hydrogen bomb. This . . . greatly deflates the arro-gance of imperialism, modern revisionism and all reactionaries. The success of China's hydrogen bomb test has further broken the nuclear monopoly of U.S. imperialism and Soviet re-visionism and dealt a telling blow at their policy of nuclear blackmail.[20]

In this statement, China has made two very significant changes. *First*, by claiming that its test has 'further broken the nuclear monopoly' of the superpowers, China apparently felt that its nuclear weapons achievement had already begun to have a direct effect on the breaking of their nuclear monopoly. *Second*, in its previous statements, China merely claimed that its nuclear tests were 'a heavy blow to the plot of the superpowers to enforce their nuclear monopoly'; but it did not mention their 'nuclear threats' or 'nuclear blackmail'. However, in this statement, China claimed that its nuclear weapon achievement was 'a telling blow at their [the superpowers'] policy of nuclear blackmail'.

After it had conducted its eighth nuclear test, China further indicated in its policy statement[21] that the test had directly affected both the superpowers' 'nuclear blackmail' and their 'nuclear threat':

> The success of the nuclear test dealt another blow to the nuclear threat and nuclear blackmail of American imperialism and Soviet revisionism. It is a big inspiration to carrying through to the end the war against the United States. . .[22]

After its ninth and tenth nuclear tests in September 1969, China further claimed:

> These new achievements in China's development of nuclear weapons serve as another heavy blow at the nuclear monopoly by U.S. imperialism and social-imperialism.[23]

Two months later, China declared herself stronger than ever.[24]

Thus, it appears that as its nuclear weapons capability has grown, China has begun to claim that its nuclear weapons development has had direct and significant effects on the 'nuclear monopoly', 'nuclear threat' and 'nuclear blackmail' by the superpowers. In other words, Communist China seems to believe that its nuclear weapons development would eventually create a situation most favourable for China to pursue its foreign policy objectives. When Communist China becomes a major nuclear power, therefore, the stalemate and self-restraints now prevailing between the superpowers would not prevail between the United States and Communist China nor between the Soviet Union and Communist China.

2. THE SUPERPOWERS AND THE ARMS RACE

Since there will not be a balance of nuclear strength and capability between Communist China and either superpower, there would not be a nuclear stalemate between them. Consequently, on the one hand, Communist China will continue to increase its nuclear force. On the other hand, the superpowers, in response to the Chinese nuclear build-up, will have to accelerate their costly and dangerous nuclear arms race far beyond their present pace in order to maintain superiority over or equality with Communist China and the other superpower.

Furthermore, the situation could become even more complicated if the Chinese nuclear weapons development entailed a chain reaction of nuclear proliferation in the international system. So far each superpower has made sure that its adversary has not developed an absolutely invulnerable nuclear system or built up an overwhelmingly superior nuclear force. However, as the number of countries possessing nuclear weapons increases, the process of balancing and adjusting would become more difficult. For example, in estimating the might of another superpower, each superpower will have to take into consideration not only the nuclear capability and military strength of its main adversary, but also the strength of its adversary's nuclear allies as well as the strength of its own allies. If the combined nuclear force of its adversaries appears to be strong enough to break the invulnerability of its second-strike force, it would have to accelerate the building of its nuclear force and military capability. Consequently, the superpowers would have to engage in a dangerous strategic nuclear arms race.

3. NEW NUCLEAR POWERS

The emergence of Communist China as a major nuclear power, because of its foreign policy objectives, could virtually force the Asian countries, notably India and Japan, to develop their own nuclear weapons. Consequently, as examined in Chapter 6, a chain reaction of nuclear proliferation would become inevitable in the international system.

It is true that there are still many disincentives, such as cost, to nuclear weapons development. However, it is important to note that the cost of nuclear weapons development for countries with small or no present nuclear facilities is by no means prohibitive.[25] As to international controls, the Partial Nuclear Test

Ban Treaty and the Nuclear Non-proliferation Treaty are not universally accepted; nor is there any agency to enforce them. Besides, as far as the Non-proliferation Treaty is concerned, parties to the treaty can withdraw from it by giving three months' notice.[26] Therefore these 'disincentives' are by no means quite so effective as they may seem. Should a country get involved in a tense local conflict, the nuclear weapons programme of its adversaries would provide it with very strong security and prestige incentives to initiate its own nuclear weapons programme. At present, many countries already possess the necessary resources and technology to start a nuclear weapons programme. In 1967, for instance, the U.S. Atomic Energy Commission reported that in addition to the present five nuclear countries, there are about forty-one countries which possess operating nuclear reactors and the technology to develop nuclear weapons.[27] In addition, at least another twenty-five countries already have non-military nuclear facilities and the industrial and technological base for nuclear weapons development. They could possibly produce such weapons in less than ten years.[28] United States Defence Secretary McNamara has also pointed out that the most advanced of the non-military nuclear countries could solve the problem of explosion technology, a necessary step in nuclear weapons development, within six months.[29] Therefore, the development of nuclear weapons by many Asian countries in response to the development of operational or major nuclear weapons by Communist China may well lead to a chain reaction of nuclear proliferation in the entire international system. As a result, the international system would face the following additional stresses which could erode the nuclear deterrence and stalemate in the present international system :

(*a*) As the number of countries possessing nuclear weapons increases, the probability of their being used would also increase. William C. Foster, Director of the U.S. Arms Control and Disarmament Agency and head of the U.S. delegation to the conference of the Eighteen-Nation Committee on Disarmament (as it was then known) at Geneva, warns that

there is the simple fact that the probability of nuclear weapons being used will almost certainly increase as the number of fingers on the triggers increase. Moreover, the increase in probability will be more than proportional to the increase in number.[30]

Henry Kissinger, now an adviser to President Nixon, argued in 1961 that 'with many countries possessing nuclear weapons, the possibility of nuclear war obviously increases'.[31] Perhaps the most illuminating statement was made by Herman Kahn when he said :

> The possibility of inadvertent war would no doubt increase not only because there would be many more weapons and missiles available, but because there will be many more organisations in existence, each with different standards of training, organisation and degrees of responsibility. The possibility of unauthorised behaviour, irresponsibility, misunderstanding of orders, or lax discipline inevitably increases. Mistakes would increase if the military or political organisation were weak or slipshod.[32]

Therefore, as the number of countries with nuclear weapons increases, the probability of their being used would also increase. (*b*) Since the new nuclear countries would not possess an invulnerable second-strike nuclear force, some of them might be tempted to launch a pre-emptive nuclear attack on their adversaries or at least their nuclear facilities to eliminate the threats or potential threats from their adversaries once and for all. (*c*) So far, there has been no threat of anonymous nuclear attack. An anonymous nuclear attack is one from unknown source or from a source difficult to identify in a very short time. At present, a nuclear attack on the United States would inevitably be attributed to the Soviet Union and vice versa. It is unlikely that France and Britain would launch such an attack. Since the attacker could be identified quickly and easily, an immediate retaliatory attack could be launched by the victim. Therefore neither superpower could expect to attack its adversary and remain undetected and unscathed. However, as the number of small independent nuclear countries increases, the source would become very difficult to identify.[33] Some nuclear countries might therefore be tempted to launch a nuclear attack on its enemies, hoping to escape detection. If such an attack were to take place in an area where tension was already quite high among various nuclear countries or where the superpowers were deeply involved, a large-scale or even a world nuclear war might become probable. On the other hand, the fear of such an attack might also tempt a nuclear country to launch a pre-emptive nuclear attack on its nuclear adversary. Furthermore, the simple fact that such an anonymous attack is possible at all could cause suspicions and tensions among national actors in the international system.

(d) In a world of nuclear power, adequate communication among countries would also become much more difficult to maintain. So far, between the superpowers, channels such as the 'hot line' have been able to help facilitate communication in time of crisis. However, 'as the number of nuclear powers increases, the amount of attention each country can pay to one rival declines'. 'Such a decline, such a "communications overload", far from leading to peace and prudence, complicates calculations.'[34] Thus, 'even if we assume that all future participants in the apocalyptic poker game will be as coolly rational as the present two players, the game itself will have become far more complex and less predictable – hence more dangerous'.[35] The new complexity would appear in the relations between various new nuclear powers, between the superpowers and those countries, and between the superpowers themselves. Consequently, chances of miscalculation and mis-escalation would become much greater. Such a situation could be extremely dangerous in the nuclear era in which decisions have to be made in split seconds.

4. RESTRAINING INFLUENCE OF THE SUPERPOWERS

When Communist China becomes a major nuclear power, the ability of the superpowers to restrain other national actors in the international system would also be significantly reduced. The following are some of the reasons and examples :

(a) Communist China no longer belongs to the Soviet camp.

It has received no military, economic or any other kind of aid or assistance since 1960. Therefore when it becomes a major nuclear power and breaks the containment imposed on it by the super-powers, neither superpower could expect to put pressure on China to restrain it from committing military mischief.

(*b*)   As mentioned earlier, the superpowers have to a significant extent restrained their camp members and other national actors from engaging in serious military conflicts. However, it would be very doubtful whether such restraints could remain intact after Communist China becomes a major nuclear power. For example, the restraints the superpowers had successfully imposed on Pakistan and India during their 1965 war might have been a failure had Communist China been a major nuclear power at that time. Discrediting U.S. deterrence and containment, Communist China might have decided not only to offer substantial military aid to Pakistan but to guarantee its security, and thus seriously complicate the situation and make settlement impossible. Also, if there is still any hope in reaching an agreement in the present Paris peace talks which have been accepted by South Vietnam and North Vietnam under the influence of the super-powers, such a hope would diminish if Communist China, after becoming a major nuclear power, felt more confident and decided to supply the North Vietnamese and Vietcong with substantial military aid or offer them guarantees of security.

The Chinese attacks on the Paris peace talks and their advocacy of revolutionary wars indicate that Communist China might take this course of action. In the Middle East, Communist China over the past years has consistently attacked Israel and supported the Arab people.[36] Much Chinese aid has been sent to Egypt, and an agreement on scientific and technical co-operation between Egypt and Communist China was signed in Cairo in January 1965.[37] The agreement was followed in April by an announcement in the authoritative Egyptian newspaper, *Al Ahram*, that Egyptian scientists were about to be sent to Communist China to receive training at China's nuclear installations.[38] When Communist China becomes a major nuclear power, its interest and involvement in the area would certainly increase. But substantial Chinese military aid to Egypt may significantly change the delicate balance of power in that area as well as render futile any efforts made by the superpowers to press the parties involved to reach a settlement. Communist China's recent support of the ousted Cambodian head of state Sihanouk – while both superpowers are tending to restrain their 'allies' in Indo-china from taking advantage of the situation – further indicates what a complicated situation the international system would have to face when Communist China becomes a major nuclear power.

Furthermore, Communist China has regarded any joint efforts made by the superpowers to maintain the *status quo* of the international system as 'plots' to maintain their 'co-domination' of the world. Such a Chinese attitude and position could have tremendous adverse effects on these efforts. For example, in view of Communist China's severe attacks on the Partial Nuclear Test Ban Treaty and the Nuclear Non-proliferation Treaty and its refusals to have anything to do with them, it is very doubtful whether many countries would still honour the treaties once Communist China becomes a major nuclear power.

(c) The willingness of the camp members and other national actors to subject themselves to the restraining powers of the superpowers would also be reduced when Communist China becomes a major nuclear power. For one thing, if the future Chinese nuclear weapons can definitely imperil the homelands of the superpowers and cause irreparable damage to them, Asian and other countries would probably not believe any commitments or guarantees offered by either superpower, doubting whether the superpowers would risk their own cities and population to come to their rescue. As Sisir Gupta has pointed out, 'if the Chinese ever succeed in building up a strategic balance with the U.S. . . . it is very questionable if it [the United States] would sacrifice Boston for Bombay or Detroit for Delhi'.[39]

Even if the superpowers' guarantees were still available and credible, the present two-camp system would still undergo some changes. For instance, if the United States decided to offer a guarantee of security to countries such as India against a potential Chinese nuclear threat, allies of America such as Japan and Thailand might feel that, since non-aligned countries enjoy virtually the same privileges and protection from the superpowers as they do, there would be little incentive for them to remain in the U.S. camp. On the other hand, if the United States refuses to offer a guarantee of security to any country aligned or non-aligned, the American allies or camp members might feel that, since they would be in the same position as the non-aligned countries, it would be unprofitable to stay in the camp. A similar situation would be true in the Soviet camp.

The situation could be more complicated and the two-camp system more unstable if many camp members decided to develop their own nuclear weapons in response to the emergence of Communist China as a major nuclear power. Of course, the precise way the development of a nuclear arsenal by a small or middle-sized power would affect its position in one of the two camps is uncertain. Much would depend on the individual situation, e.g. the way in which it attempted to exploit its nuclear weapons, the reactions of other countries, etc. Thus, in the case of Britain, the strains of proliferation may not at all impair its relations with the United States; but the same cannot be said in the cases of Communist China and France, whose relations with the superpowers have deteriorated.

Nuclear proliferation in the international system tends to have a negative impact on the relations between the superpowers and their camp members. In the case of a new nuclear country, the possession of nuclear weapons may make it feel that it is an 'independent' country and therefore should enjoy a greater degree of autonomy. Consequently, it may feel that it can make key decisions for itself without the consent of the superpower. As Hans J. Morgenthau observes, 'a nation will shun alliances if it believes that it is strong enough to hold its own unaided'.[40] R. C. Snyder also observes that the possession of nuclear weapons might lead to intra-bloc tension within an alliance system.[41] Consequently, there would inevitably be disruptive effects on the present two-camp system.

On the other hand, the superpowers might decide to shun alliances or small nuclear camp members if they felt that the burden of military or political commitments appeared too heavy to bear or if they felt there was a great danger of getting involved in a local nuclear conflict.

As the superpowers and other national actors further alienate each other in a world of nuclear powers, the ability of the superpowers to restrain their camp members and other national actors would inevitably be reduced.

5. NON-ALIGNED ACTORS

When Communist China becomes a major nuclear power, many countries, especially those in Asia, might decide or be forced to join the Chinese camp, or become constant supporters of Chinese foreign policy. Consequently, the size, strength and effectiveness of the non-aligned actors in the international system would be greatly reduced.

6. THE UNIVERSAL ACTOR

The reduction in size and significance of the non-aligned actors would also seriously affect the functioning of the United Nations as a 'preventive diplomacy' or 'preventive security' agency in the international system. Furthermore, these countries have so far regarded the United Nations not only as a significant organisation for the maintenance of world peace, but as the protector of their integrity and independence. As Francis O. Wilcox explains,

the great powers do not need the United Nations; at any rate, they can defend themselves in time of peril. Similarly, the aligned countries, associated with the Soviet Union in the Warsaw Pact and other pacts, and with the Western powers in NATO, CENTO, SEATO, the Rio pact and other defense agreements, have certain assurances against aggression and are less inclined to turn to the United Nations for protection. But the non-aligned countries, without the protective umbrella of the United Nations, would be standing relatively unshielded and alone in a world where aggressors could often take their tool.

To the smaller nations, and the non-aligned countries in particular, the United Nations has tremendous value. It was designed to protect their independence and integrity and to help them raise their standards of living. It is also a center where a smaller state, without much status or prestige, can greatly enhance its influence by joining with other states to realise common policy objectives. Even more important, membership in the U.N. is a symbol of each country's standing and dignity as a sovereign entity.[42]

However, when these non-aligned countries become nuclear countries in response to Chinese nuclear development, they would feel that since they have nuclear weapons, they do not have to depend on the Organisation for the maintenance of their independence and sovereignty. Should they get involved in a local conflict, they would think that nuclear weapons could be used as a last resort for final victory or for a showdown with their adversaries. Consequently, their willingness to accept a U.N. mediation would significantly decrease. In this regard, United States Secretary of Defence McNamara seems to be correct when he says that if armed conflicts were to occur between countries without nuclear weapons, the international agencies of peace-keeping and conflict adjustment could often be able to operate effectively; but with countries possessing nuclear weapons, these peace-keeping activities may become impossible.[43] Although the word 'impossible' may be too strong, the task of peace-keeping would certainly become much more difficult.

When Communist China emerges as a major nuclear power, the international political system, i.e. the 'loose bipolar system', will become very unstable. While the addition of a third major nuclear power would inevitably change the basic structural pattern of the international system, with Communist China as the third major national actor, there will be more than simply minor structural changes. The above discussion clearly indicates that when Communist China becomes a major nuclear power, because of its foreign policy objectives and its relations with other national actors in the international system, the stability of the system would significantly diminish, if not disappear. Several serious changes in the characteristics of the system – e.g. the decreasing restraining power of the superpowers over other national actors; the diminishing effectiveness of the present nuclear stalemate and nuclear deterrence; the reduction in the functions and significance of the universal actor, i.e. the United Nations, and of the non-aligned actors in the international system – would take place.

In other words, the system of national actors or groups of national actors that are essential to maintain the stability of the international system would be irreversibly changed : (1) There would be three major national actors, leading to the consequences already discussed; (2) the two-camp system would be further eroded or would disappear completely; (3) the number of non-aligned actors would be significantly reduced; and (4) while the universal actor might continue to play a part, its functions and significance would be greatly reduced.

Notes

CHAPTER 1

1. Hans Thirring, 'Can We Sleep Soundly in the Shadow of the Hydrogen Bomb?' *Bulletin of the Atomic Scientists*, II (Feb 1955) 59–61.

2. Stanley Hoffman, *The State of War: Essays in the Theory and Practice of International Politics* (New York: F. A. Praeger, 1965) p. 237. See also Thomas C. Schelling, 'The Threat that Leaves Something to Chance', in his *The Strategy of Conflict* (New York: Oxford University Press, 1963) pp. 187–204.

3. See Stanley Hoffman, *The State of War*, pp. 233–4. See also Ciro Elliott Zoppo, 'Nuclear Technology, Multipolarity, and International Stability', *World Politics*, 16, no. 4 (July 1966) 585. See also George Schwarzenberger, 'Beyond Power Politics', *The Year Book of World Affairs 1965*, p. 224.

4. Ciro Elliott Zoppo, 'Nuclear Technology, Multipolarity, and International Stability', p. 585.

5. Hans J. Morgenthau, 'Has Atomic War Really Become Impossible?', *Bulletin of the Atomic Scientists* (Jan 1956) pp. 7–9.

6. These drastic changes may or may not be carried out by direct military force.

7. Stanley Hoffman, 'Nuclear Proliferation and World Politics', *A World of Nuclear Powers?*, ed. Alastair Buchan (Englewood Cliffs, N.J.: Prentice-Hall, 1966) p. 93.

8. See Robert L. Rothstein, *Alliances and Small Powers* (New York: Columbia University Press, 1968) pp. 238 ff.

9. See Bruce M. Russett, 'Discovering Voting Groups in the United Nations', *American Political Science Review* (June 1966) pp. 327 ff.

10. See Hayward R. Alker Jr. and Bruce M. Russett, *World Politics in the General Assembly* (New Haven: Yale University Press, 1965).

11. Bruce M. Russett, 'Discovering Voting Groups in the United Nations' *American Political Science Review* (June 1966) pp. 327 ff.

12. See Earnst Lefever, 'Nehru, Nasser, and Nkrumah on Neutralism', *Neutralism and Non-alignment*, ed. Laurence Martin (New York: F. A. Praeger, 1962).

13. Inis L. Claude Jr., *Swords into Plowshares* (New York: Random, 1971) pp. 312 ff.

14. Ibid. p. 332.

15. For further discussion on systems theory, see for example Stanley Hoffman, 'International System and International Law', *World Politics*, 14, no. 1 (Oct 1961) p. 207; David Easton, *A Framework for Political Analysis* (Englewood, Cliffs, N.J.: Prentice-Hall, 1965); Morton A. Kaplan, *System and Process in International Politics*, Science Edition (New York: John Wiley, 1964); Charles A. McClelland, *Theory and the International System* (New York; Macmillan Co., 1966).

16. Stanley Hoffman, *The State of War, p.* 248.

17. Herman Kahn, *Thinking about the Unthinkable,* (New York: Horizon Press, 1962) p. 223.

CHAPTER 2

1. Robert A. Scalapino, 'The Cultural Revolution and Chinese Foreign Policy', *Current Scene: Developments in Mainland China*, VI, no. 13 (1 Aug 1968) 2.

2. For similar models, see Norton Ginsburg, 'On the Chinese Perception of a World Order', *China in Crisis*, 2, ed. Tang Tsou (Chicago: University of Chicago Press, 1968) 73–91; John K. Fairbank, 'China's World Order', *Encounter*, 27 (Dec 1966) 14–15. See also 'The Geography of Mainland China: A Concise Sketch', *Current Scene*, VII, no. 17 (1 Sept 1969) 1–21.

3. Sun Yat-sen, *San Min Chu I (Three People's Principles)* (Taipei, Taiwan: Cheng Chung, 1954) p. 6.

4. Chiang Kai-shek, *China's Destiny and Chinese Economic Theory* (New York: Roy Publication, 1947) pp. 34, 79.

5. Mao Tse-tung, 'The Chinese Revolution and the Chinese Communist Party', 15 Dec 1939 version, *Current Background*, no. 135 (10 Nov 1951), cit. A. Doak Barnett, *Communist China and Asia: A Challenge to American Policy* (New York: Random House, 1960) p. 79.

6. Mao Tse-tung, speech on 21 Sept 1949, *China Digest* (5 Oct 1949).

7. Cit. Robert S. Elegant, *The Centre of the World: Communism and the Mind of China* (London: Methuen, 1963) p. x.

8. Hans J. Morgenthau, 'The United States and China', *China in Crisis*, 2, 95.

9. For Communist China's determination to 'liberate' Taiwan, see for example *Hung Ch'i (Red Flag)*, no. 9 (27 Aug 1969) 24–8.

10. For details see W. E. Griffith, 'Sino-Soviet Relations 1964–5, *China Quarterly*, no. 25 (Jan-Mar 1966), 28–30. See also 8 October 1969, *Peking Review*, no. 41 (10 Oct 1969). For a map with detailed illustration, see *People's Daily, Kwan-ming Daily*, 8 Oct 1969.

11. Edgar Snow, *Red Star over China*, rev. ed. (New York: Garden City Publishing Co., 1939) pp. 88–9.

12. See Chiang Kai-shek, *China's Destiny and Chinese Economic Theory*, pp. 77–8.

13. *Peking Review*, no. 22 (30 May 1969) 7.

14. *Peking Review*, no. 38 (19 Sept 1969) 27.

15. *Peking Review*, no. 47 (21 Nov 1969) 28.

16. See for example Tomokatsu Matsumara, 'How Likely A Head-on Collision?', *Atlas*, 15 no. 2 (Feb 1968) 38. Matsumara is a leading Japanese expert on China.

17. C. P. Fitzgerald, *The Chinese View of Their Place in the World* (New York: Oxford University Press, 1964) pp. 18–19.

18. Mao's traditional thinking is derived from many Chinese classics such as *Tales of the Three Kingdoms, All Men Are Brothers*.

19. *Polemic of the General Line of the International Communist Movement* (Peking: Foreign Languages Press, 1963) p. 24.

20. Statement by the Spokesman of the Chinese Government – A Comment on the Soviet Government's Statement of 3 Aug, 15 Aug 1963 in *People of the World, Unite, for the Complete, Thorough, Total and Resolute Prohibition and Destruction of Nuclear Weapons* (Peking: Foreign Languages Press, 1963) p. 24.

21. Statement by the Spokesman of the Chinese Government – A Comment on the Soviet Government's Statement of 21 Aug, 1 Sept 1963, in *People of the World . . .*, 49.

22. Mao Tse-tung, *Selected Works*, vi (Peking: Foreign Languages Press, 1963) 97–101.

23. 'On Mao Tse-tung's Talk with a Group of Japanese Socialists', *Pravda*, 2 Sept 1964, repr. in *International Affairs* (Moscow) no. 10 (Oct 1964) 80–5.

24. Mao Tse-tung, *On People's Democratic Dictatorship*, July 1949 (Peking: Foreign Languages Press, 1952) p. 10.

25. 'Source Material: Several Important Problems concerning the Current International Situation', no. 17 (25 Apr 1961), *Bulletin of Activities* or *Kung-tso T'ung-hsu* (*Work Correspondances*), in *The Politics of the Chinese Red Army*, ed. J. Chester Cheng (Stanford, Calif.: Stanford University, 1966) p. 481.

26. Editorial, *People's Daily*, 31 Mar 1964.

27. Ibid.

28. *Peking Review*, nos. 10, 11 (15 Mar 1963) 16–17.

29. See 'Long Live the Victory of People's War', *Peking Review*, no. 36 (3 Sept 1965) 9–31.

30. Ibid., p. 24.

31. *Chinese Communist Affairs Bi-Monthly*, 2, no. 2 (Apr 1965) 16. For similar views expressed by the Communist Chinese, see also 'Source Material: Several Important Problems Concerning the Current International Situation', pp. 480–7. See also Tung Chi-ping and Humphrey Evans, *The Thought Revolution* (New York: Coward–McCann, 1966) p. 223.

32. Ibid.

33. Mao Tse-tung, 'Problems of War and Strategy', 6 Nov 1938, *Selected Military Writings* (Peking: Foreign Languages Press, 1963) pp. 242, 269.

34. Ibid., 272–3.

35. Ibid., 267.

36. Mao Tse-tung, 'Report of An Investigation into the Peasant Movement in Hunan', *Selected Works*, 1 (London: Lawrence and Wishart, 1955), 27. See also his *Selected Works*, ii (Peking: People's Press, 1961) 600.

37. Editorial, *People's Daily*, 22 Oct 1963.

38. Sung Tu, 'Answers to Reader's Questions on War and Peace', *China Youth (Chung-kuo Ch'ing-nien)* no. 4 (16 Feb 1960), cit. in Vidya Prakash Dutt, *China and the World*, p. 88.

39. *Peaceful Co-existence – Two Diametrically Opposed Politics* (Peking: Foreign Languages Press, 1963) p. 5.

40. Hans J. Morgenthau, 'The Vietnam Crisis and China', *Bulletin of the Atomic Scientists* (June 1965) p. 27.

41. Walter B. Wentz, *Nuclear Proliferation* (Washington : Public Affairs Press, 1968) p. 50.

42. For details, see Morton H. Halperin and Dwight H. Perkins, *Communist China and Arms Control* (Cambridge, Mass.: Frederick A. Praeger for Harvard University, 1965) pp. 17 ff.

43. A. Doak Barnett, *Communist China and Asia*, p. 68.

44. Morton H. Halperin and Dwight H. Perkins, *Communist China and Arms Control.*, p. 1.

45. Franz H. Michael and George E. Taylor, *The Far East in the Modern World* (New York: Holt, Rinehart & Winston, 1964); H. Arthur Steiner, 'The Mainsprings of Chinese Communist Foreign Policy', *American Journal of International Law*, xliv, no. 1 (Jan 1950); Richard L. Walker, *The Continuing Struggles: Communist China and the Free World* (New York: Athene, 1958).

46. Richard Harris, 'China and the World', *International Affairs* (London) 35 no. 2 (Apr 1959) 162.

47. Abraham M. Halpern, 'China in the Postwar World', *China Quarterly*, no. 21 (Jan–Mar 1965) 43.

48. Allen S. Whiting, 'Foreign Policy of Communist China', in *Foreign Policy in World Politics*, ed. Roy C. Macridis (Englewood Cliffs, N.J.: Prentice-Hall, 1967) p. 296.

49. Robert A. Scalapino, 'The Foreign Policy of the People's Republic of China,' in *Foreign Policies in A World of Change*, ed. Joseph E. Black and Kenneth W. Thompson (New York: Harper & Sons, 1963) pp. 549–90; 'The Cultural Revolution and Chinese Foreign Policy', *Current Scene*, vi, no. 13 (1 Aug 1968) 1–15; Harold C. Hinton, *Communist China in World Politics*; A. Doak Barnett, *Communist China and Asia*.

50. A study of the causes of the Sino-Soviet conflict involves the consideration of both the ideological and national interests of Communist China.

Ideologically, Communist China is convinced that the Soviet Union's recent 'revisionist' policy towards the 'imperialist countries' notably the United States, has weakened the cause of Communism. The Soviet Union's reluctance to support revolutionary wars is also regarded by Communist China as a betrayal of 'socialism'. At the same time, the border disputes between the two countries involve their vital national interests. In addition, Communist China has been discontented with the Soviet Union's lack of support in cases such as the Quemoy crisis in 1958. Furthermore Soviet aid for India during the Sino-Indian war annoyed and disheartened Communist China. The Soviet Union's decision not to help Communist China to become an independent nuclear country has also been regarded by Communist China as detrimental to the Chinese national interest. The Sino-Soviet conflict involves more problems and differences than these; but these examples may indicate the 'mixed' nature of the conflict. Similarly, in the Sino-American conflict, in addition to Communist China's ideological hostility towards 'imperialists', the American 'occupation' of Taiwan and its military bases around China are regarded as threats to China's vital national interests. It would therefore be a mistake to try to trace the causes of these conflicts to either ideology or national interest alone.

CHAPTER 3

1. *People's Daily*, 2 Aug 1963; *Peking Review*, no. 32 (2 Aug 1963) 8.

2. 'Statement by the Spokesman of the Chinese Government – A Comment on the Soviet Government's Statement of 3 Aug', 15 Aug 1963, in *People of the World, Unite* (Peking: Foreign Languages Press, 1963) p. 24.

3. Editorial, *People's Daily*, 22 Oct 1964, in *SCMP*, no. 3325.

4. Kuo Mo-jo is President of the Chinese Academy of Science. For details of his proposal, see *NCNA*, 4 Feb 1958; *SCMP*, no. 1708 (7 Feb 1958) 41–2.

5. *Peking Review*, no. 31 (2 Aug 1963) 8.

6. *Peking Review*, no. 36 (6 Sept 1963).

7. *Peking Review*, no. 44 (30 Oct 1964) 6–7.

8. 'Premier Chou Cables Government Heads of the World', *Peking Review*, no. 43 (23 Oct 1964) 6.

9. Editorial, *People's Daily*, 22 Nov 1964.

10. *U.N. Documents*, A/5174, Annex II (1962) 78. However, many American writers argue that a 'no-first-use pledge' is highly desirable. See for example Bernard T. Feld, 'A Pledge: No First Use', *Bulletin of the Atomic Scientists* (May 1967) p. 48.

11. *New York Times*, 19 Oct 1964.

12. *New York Times*, 22 Oct 1964.

13. *ENDC Document*, ENDC/167 (1966).

14. See for example *People's Daily*, 7 Apr 1958.

15. *People's Daily*, 22 Dec 1961.

16. 'Statement by the Spokesman of the Chinese Government – A Comment

on the Soviet Government's Statement of 3 Aug', 15 Aug 1963, in *People of the World . . .* , 22.

17. *People's Daily*, 19 July 1963.   For details see also *People's Daily*, 29 July 1–5 Aug, 10 Aug and 15 Aug 1963.

18. Editorial, *People's Daily*, 22 Oct 1964.

19. 'Break the Nuclear Monopoly, Eliminate Nuclear Weapons', p. 15. See also 'Statement of the Government of the People's Republic of China', 16 Oct 1964, in *Break the Nuclear Monopoly . . .*, pp. 1–5.

CHAPTER 4

1. *NCNA*, 18 Jan 1958, in *SCMP*, no. 1696 (22 Jan 1958), 34–5, cit. Alice Langley Hsieh, *Communist China's Strategy in the Nuclear Era*, p. 101.

2. Robert Guillain, 'Ten Years of Secrecy', *Bulletin of the Atomic Scientists* (Feb 1967) pp. 24–5.

3. 'Statement by the Spokesman of the Chinese Government – A Comment on the Soviet Government's Statement of 21 August', *People of the World, Unite, for the Complete, Thorough, Total and Resolute Prohibition and Destruction of Nuclear Weapons* (Peking: Foreign Languages Press, 1963) pp. 37–8.

4. 'Statement by the Spokesman of the Chinese Government – A Comment on the Soviet Government's Statement of 3 August', in *People of the world . . .*, p. 30.

5. *New York Times*, 22 Aug 1963. For Alice Langley Hsieh's comment, see her *Communist China's Strategy in the Nuclear Era* (Englewood Cliffs, N.J.: Prentice-Hall, 1962) p. 100.

6. *Communist Chinese Affairs Monthly*, 8, no. 4 (31 May 1965), 12.

7. *New York Times*, 29 Oct 1963.

8. *Communist Chinese Affairs Monthly*, 8, no. 4 (31 May 1965), 12.

9. *New York Times*, 17 Oct 1964.

10. *New York Times*, 4 Dec 1964.

11. Ibid.

12. *New York Times*, 15 May 1965.

13. *Chinese Communist Affairs Bi-Monthly* (Apr 1968) p. 6. See also *New York Times*, 21 May 1966 and 22 May 1966.

14. *New York Times*, 28 Oct 1966.

15. *New York Times*, 28 Oct 1966.

16. *NCNA*, 27 Oct. 1966.

17. *New York Times*, 29 and 31 Dec 1966.

18. *New York Times*, 29 Dec 1966.

19. *New York Times*, 10 Sept 1967.

20. *New York Times*, 18 June 1967.

21. *Peking Review*, no. 41 (7 Oct 1966) 31.

22. *NCNA*, 28 Dec 1969.

23. *Peking Review*, no. 41 (10 Oct 1969) 22.

24. See *New York Times*, 29 Apr 1965. Many other experts agreed that Communist China apparently assembled its first bomb with more skill than the United States and the Soviet Union had done in their first efforts: *New York Times*, 21 Oct 1965.

25. *New York Times*, 18 June and 3 Aug 1967.

26. *New York Times*, 2 Jan 1967.

27. *New York Times*, 15 May 1965.

28. See for example Joseph E. Fix III, 'China – the Nuclear Threat', *Air University Quarterly Review* (Mar–Apr 1966) pp. 28–9.

29. For details see John Lindbeck, 'An Isolationist Science Policy', *Bulletin of the Atomic Scientists* (Feb 1969) p. 68. See also W. L. Ryan and S. Summerlin, *China Cloud*, p. 188; C. Y. Cheng, *Scientific and Engineering Manpower in Communist China*, 1949–63, National Science Foundation (Washington: U.S. Government Printing Office, 1965).

30. 'Is Red China's H-bomb A Product of the West?', *Atlas*, 16 (Dec 1968) 22–24.

31. John Lindbeck, 'An Isolationist Science Policy', p. 68.

32. W. L. Ryan and S. Summerlin, *China Cloud: America's Tragedy and Cina's Rise to Nuclear Power* (Boston: Little, Brown, 1968) p. 188.

33. Other top scientists include Peng Huang-wu, Kuo Yung-huai, Chang Chia-hua, etc.
For details see W. L. Ryan and S. Summerlin, *China Cloud*, p. 188; *New York Times*, 25 Oct 1964, 8 Jan 1967.

34. China appears to have produced ample supplies of lithium ore concentrates, beryllium concentrates, borax wolfram concentrates, piezoelectric quartz, mercury, tantalum-biobium concentrates, molybdenum concentrates and tin, all of which are needed for nuclear weapons development. For details see John A. Berberet, *Science and Technology in Communist China* (Santa Barbara, Calif.: General Electric Co., Technical Military Planning Operation, 1960).

35. 'Is Red China's H-bomb A Product of the West?', p. 22.

36. Ibid.

37. 'Chinese Communist Eight Nuclear Tests Viewed after the Eighth Blast', *Chinese Communist Affairs Monthly*, II, no. 12 (1 Feb 1969) 14. See also *Communist Chinese Affairs Monthly* no. 6 (31 July 1965) 22. See also ibid., 7 no. 11 (31 Dec 1964) 89–90.

38. Leonard Beaton, 'The Chinese Bomb: the Institute for Strategic Studies View', *Survival*, 7, no. 1 (Jan–Feb 1965) 2–4. See also *New York Times*, 2 Nov 1966.

39. See also *The Military Balance 1970–1971* and *Strategic Survey 1970* (London: The Institute for Strategic Studies, 1971).

40. For details see Alice Langley Hsieh, 'Sino-Soviet Nuclear Dialogue', *Bulletin of the Atomic Scientists* (Jan 1965) pp. 16–21.

41. For Secretary of Defence Melvin R. Laird's statement before a joint session of the Senate Armed Services and Appropriations Committees, see *Fiscal Year* 1971 *Defense Program and Budget* (Washington: U.S. Government Printing Office, 1970).

42. Morton H. Halperin, *China and the Bomb* (New York: F. A. Praeger, 1965) p. 154.

43. For discussion on Communist China as a major nuclear power, see Chapter 7 below.

44. Quoted in *The Times* (London), 4 May 1964.

45. News dispatch from Hong Kong, *Edmonton Journal*, 17 Feb 1970.

46. See *Communist Chinese Affairs Bi-Monthly* (Apr 1968) pp. 8–9.

47. *New York Times*, 28 Oct 1966.

48. *New York Times*, 16 Dec 1965.

49. *New York Times*, 30 Oct 1967.

50. *New York Times*, 22 Jan 1967.

51. *New York Times*, 20 June 1967.

52. For Professor Hilsman's statement, see *New York Times*, 19 Nov 1964.

53. *New York Times*, 29 Dec 1966.

54. *New York Times*, 29 Dec 1966.

55. *New York Times*, 12 Jan 1967.

56. See *Fiscal Year* 1971 *Defense Program and Budget*.

57. News dispatch from Washington, *Edmonton Journal,* 7 Jan 1970.

58. J. I. Coffey, 'The Chinese and Ballistic Missile Defence', *Bulletin of the Atomic Scientists* (Dec 1965) p. 17.

59. See *Fiscal Year* 1971 *Defense Program and Budget*.

60. For details see *New York Times*, 26 Apr 1970 and *Hsinhua News Agency* (*NCNA*) news despatch, 25 Apr 1970. However, since they were not nuclear tests, they will not be discussed in length.

CHAPTER 5

1. 'Open Letter from C.P.S.U. C.C. to Party Organisations and all Communists of the Soviet Union', *Pravda*, 14 July; *Soviet News*, no. 4872 (17 July 1963), 29–43, rep. in William E. Griffith, *The Sino-Soviet Rift* (Cambridge, Mass.: The M.I.T. Press, 1963), document 3, 298–9.

2. Ernst Henri, 'Mao Tse-tung Gazes upon Five Continents', *Atlas* (14 Dec 1967) 15.

3. Tsui Chiu-yen, 'Peiping's Design in Exploding its Nuclear Device', *Issues and Studies*, 1, no. 6 (Mar 1965) 18; 'Soviet Government Statement – Reply to Statement Made by the Chinese Government', 21 Sept 1963 *Soviet News*, nos. 4896 and 4897 (23–4 Sept 1963), 159–74, rep. in William E. Griffith, *The Sino-Soviet Rift*, document 12, 445.

4. 'Soviet Government Statement, 21 August 1963', *Soviet News*, no. 4885

(21 Aug 1963), 103–9, rep. in William E. Griffith, *The Sino-Soviet Rift*, document 8, 366.

5. See Raymond L. Garthoff, 'A Soviet Critique of China's "Total Strategy", *The Reporter*, xxxiv, no. 10 (19 May 1966) 49.

6. See 'Statement by the Spokesman of the Chinese Government – A Comment on the Soviet Government's Statement of 21 August', 1 Sept 1963. *Peking Review*, no. 36 (6 Sept 1963), See also 'Long Live Leninism!' *Red Flag* (16 Apr 1960) and *People's Daily*, editorial, 31 Dec 1963.

7. Ibid. See also *Peking Review*, no. 44 (1 Nov 1963), 19–20.

8. 'China is Determined to Make All Necessary Sacrifices for the Defeat of U.S. Imperialism', *Peking Review*, no. 41 (8 Oct 1965) 14.

9. 'Open Letter from C.P.S.U. C.C. to Party Organisations and All Communists of the Soviet Union, p. 299.

10. Mao Tse-tung, 'On Protracted War', *Selected Military Writings of Mao Tse-tung* (Peking: Foreign Languages Press, 1963) p. 239. See also his *Selected Works*, ii (London: Lawrence & Wishart, 1954) 192.

11. See 'Speech of Comrade Yeh Chien-ying at the Training Meeting of the Military Affairs Commission', *Bulletin of Activities*, no. 10 (20 Feb 1961), in *The Politics of the Chinese Red Army*, ed. J. Chester Cheng (Stanford, Calif.: The Hoover Institution on War, Revolution and Peace, Stanford University, 1966) 249–55.

12. 'Statement of the Government of the People's Republic of China', 16 Oct 1964, in *Break the Nuclear Monopoly, Eliminate Nuclear Weapons* (Peking: Foreign Languages Press, 1965) p. 3. See also *People's Daily*, 31 Dec 1964.

13. *Kuang-ming Jih-Pao*, 23 Nov 1954, in *SCMP*, no. 934 (24 Nov 1954) 13–14.

14. See 'Comrade Yeh Chien-ying's Summing-up Report to the First Conference of the Manuals Review Board of the Military Affairs Commission (Brief)', *Bulletin of Activities*, no. 26 (13 July 1961), in *The Politics of the Chinese Red Army*, ed. J. Chester Cheng, pp. 651–7.

15. 'Speech of Comrade Yeh Chien-ying at the Training Meeting of the Military Affairs Commission,' 249–55.

16. 'Chou En-lai, Interview with Agence France Presse, 3 Feb 1964' *Peking Review*, no. 7 (14 Feb 1964) 16.

17. See 'Soviet Government Statement – Reply to Statement Made by the Chinese Government, 21 Sept 1963', pp. 454–7.

18. *Peking Review*, no. 47 (27 Nov 1963), 11–12.

19. *Peking Review*, no. 25 (21 June 1963) 14.

20. 'Long Live the Victory of People's War', *Peking Review* (3 Sept 1965) pp. 9–31. The Communist Chinese claim that they had never received any foreign aid during the Chinese civil war is obviously untrue.

21. Ibid. See also Mao Tse-tung, 'Smash Chiang Kai-shek's Offensive by a War of Self-Defense', 20 July 1946, *Selected Works*, iv (Peking: Foreign Languages Press, 1961) 91.

22. Mao Tse-tung, 'On the Tactics of Fighting Japanese Imperialism', 27 Dec 1935, *Selected Works*, I (New York: International Publishers), 173.

23. Mao Tse-tung, 'On the People's Democratic Dictatorship', 30 June 1949, *Selected Works*, IV (Peking: Foreign Languages Press, 1961) 416.

24. 'Source Material: Several Important Problems Concerning the Current International Situation', *Bulletin of Activities*, no. 17 (25 Apr 1961), in *The Politics of the Chinese Red Army*, ed. J. Chester Cheng, p. 483.

25. 'Statement by the Spokesman of the Chinese Government – A Comment on the Soviet Government's Statement of 21 Aug', 1 Sept 1963, in *People of the World Unite, for the Complete, Thorough, Total and Resolute Prohibition and Destruction of Nuclear Weapons* (Peking: Foreign Languages Press, 1963), p. 50.

26. *Peking Review*, no. 47 (27 Nov 1963).

27. See 'Long Live the Victory of People's War'.

28. See *Peking Review*, no. 47 (27 Nov 1963).

29. See for example *People's Daily*, 8 Aug 1958.

30. 'Laos: The Chinese Highwaymen', p. 47. See also *New York Times*, 6 May 1966; *Edmonton Journal*, 24 Mar 1969, Los Angeles Times Service from Saigon; *Edmonton Journal*, 3 Sept 1969, New York Times Service; for other aspects of Chinese aid to North Vietnam and Vietcongs, see *New York Times*, 17 Jan 1965; *Edmonton Journal*, 13 Apr 1970.

31. See Yeh Chien-yin's speech on 27 July 1955, *NCNA*, 27 July 1955, *Current Background*, no. 347 (23 Aug 1955) 29–31.

32. 'Break the Nuclear Monopoly, Eliminate Nuclear Weapons', editorial, *People's Daily*, 22 Oct 1964. In this statement, Communist China had apparently exaggerated the 'nuclear threat' of the United States. For one thing, the United States does not have these 'nuclear bases' in Asia.

33. *Peking Review*, no. 6 (5 Feb 1965) 19.

34. *Peking Review*, no. 41 (8 Oct 1965) 14. See also 'Peking's Obsession: Nuclear War with the U.S. Is Inevitable – Red China's Foreign Minister Plainly Lays Out An Ominous View', *The National Observer*, 28 Nov 1966. p. 26.

CHAPTER 6

1. For text of Johnson's statement see *New York Times*, 17 Oct 1964.

2. See for example *New York Times*, 15 May 1965 and 4 July 1967.

3. For a detailed analysis see 'Ban on Nuclear Proliferation and Peiping's H-bomb Test', *Wen-ti yi yuan-chu*, 7, no. 1 (Oct 1967), 54–6.

4. Arthur J. Godberg, 'U.S. Calls for Prompt Endorsement by the General Assembly of the Draft Treaty on the Non-proliferation of Nuclear Weapons', *The Non-proliferation of Nuclear Weapons*, Department of State Publication 8385 (Washington: U.S. Government Printing Office, 1968) p. 8.

5. *U.N. Document* A/C.1/PV.1441, 3 Nov 1966.

6. See *New York Times*, 18 Oct, 24 Oct, 24 Nov and 5 Dec 1964.

7. Raymond Aron, *The Great Debate* (Garden City, N.Y.: Doubleday, 1965) p. 62.

8. Stanley Hoffman, 'Nuclear Proliferation and World Politics', in *A World of Nuclear Powers?*, ed. Alastair Buchan (Englewood Cliffs, N.J.: Prentice-Hall, 1966) p. 113.

9. Stanley Hoffman, 'Nuclear Proliferation and World Politics', p. 114.

10. See Sisir Gupta, 'The Indian Dilemma', *A World of Nuclear Powers?*, pp. 62–3.

11. Robert L. Rothstein, *On Nuclear Proliferation* (New York: Columbia University, 1966) p. 60.

12. See Thomas C. Schelling, *The Strategy of Conflict* (New York: Oxford University Press, 1963) pp. 6, 119, 138, 192 and especially 187 ff.

13. For further discussion, see Chapter 7 below.

14. 'Defending the Motherland! Safeguarding World Peace: China Successfully Explodes Its First Atom Bomb', Chinese Government Statement, 16 Oct 1964, Special Supplement in *Peking Review*, no. 42 (16 Oct 1964) ii–iii.

15. 'Break the Nuclear Monopoly, Eliminate Nuclear Weapons', editorial, *People's Daily*, 22 Oct 1954. Repr. and trans. in *Break the Nuclear Monopoly, Eliminate Nuclear Weapons* (Peking: Foreign Languages Press, 1965) p. 15.

16. China, in her statement after her second nuclear test in 1965, did not mention the effects of her test on revolutionary wars.

17. 'China Successfully Conducts Nuclear Explosion Containing Thermo-Nuclear Material', *Hsinhua* (*NCNA*) dispatch, 9 May 1966. See also *Peking Review*, 13 May 1966).

18. Alice L. Hsieh, foreword to the Japanese edition of *Communist China's Strategy in the Nuclear Era: Implications of the Chinese Nuclear Detonations* (Santa Monica, Calif.: Rand Corp., 1965) p. 6.

19. *New York Times*, 31 May 1966.

20. 'China Successfully Conducted Guided Missile-Nuclear Weapon Test', *Hsinhua* (*NCNA*) dispatch, 27 Oct 1966. See also *Peking Review*, special supplement 28 Oct 1966.

21. 'China Successfully Conducts New Nuclear Explosion', *Hsinhua* (*NCNA*) dispatch, 28 Dec 1966. See also *Peking Review*, 1 Jan 1967.

22. 'China's First Hydrogen Bomb Successfully Exploded', *Hsinhua* (*NCNA*) dispatch, 17 Jan 1967. See also *Peking Review*, 23 June 1967.

23. *Hsinhua* (*NCNA*) dispatch, 28 Dec 1968.

24. 'China Victoriously Conducts a Nuclear Hydrogen Bomb Explosion, Successfully Conducts the First Underground Nuclear Test', *Hsinhua* (*NCNA*) dispatch, 4 Oct 1969. See also *Peking Review*, 10 Oct 1969. Apparently because space satellites are strictly speaking not 'nuclear weapons', Communist China did not directly mention their military and political implications after its 1970 and 1971 tests.

25. See for example *New York Times*, 18 Oct 1964, 17 May 1965, 11 and 12 May 1966, 30 Dec 1967. See also *Peking Review*, no. 45 (4 Nov 1966), 27; no. 47 (21 Nov 1969), 18–19.

26. See *Peking Review*, no. 47 (21 Nov 1969) 10–11.

27. See *Hindu*, 29 Oct 1964. See also W. I. Ryan and S. Summerlin, *China Cloud: America's Tragedy and China's Rise to Nuclear Power* (Boston: Little, Brown, 1968) p. 190.

28. This statement was made in 1966. See W. L. Ryan and S. Summerlin, *China Cloud*, p. 241.

29. See M. R. Masani, 'The Challenge of the Chinese Bomb–II', *India Quarterly*, xxi, no. 1 (Jan–Mar 1965) 23. See also *The Times* (London), 5 Dec. 1964.

30. See 'World Reactions to the Chinese Nuclear Bomb', *Foreign Affairs Reports*, vol. 14, no. 1 (Jan 1965) 9.

31. See *New York Times*, 17 Oct 1964, 18 Oct 1964, 5 Dec 1964, 15 May 1965, 4 Nov 1966.

32. This statement was made by Sato in 1965, cit. Kei Wakaizumi, 'The Problem for Japan', in *A World of Nuclear Powers?*, ed. Alastair Buchan, p. 82.

33. See for example *Peking Review*, no. 22 (27 May 1966) 38; no. 45 (4 Nov 1966) 27.

34. Sisir Gupta, 'The Indian Dilemma', pp. 61–2.

35. *People of the World, Unite, for the Complete, Thorough, Total and Resolute Prohibition and Destruction of Nuclear Weapons* (Peking: Foreign Languages Press, 1963) p. 5.

36. Editorial, *People's Daily*, 22 Nov 1964.

37. *Peking Review*, 27 Nov 1964, pp. 16–18. See also ibid., 18 Dec 1964, pp. 6–8.

38. *Peking Review*, no. 38 (19 Sept 1969) 27.

39. *Communist Chinese Affairs Monthly*, 7, no. 11 (31 Dec 1964) 85–90.

40. For details, see above, p. 40.

41. Alice Langley Hsieh, 'China's Secret Military Papers: Military Doctrine and Strategy', *China Quarterly*, no. 18 (Apr–June 1964) 98, 87. See also 'Résumé of Discussion at the Ground Force Training Conference Concerning the Implementation of the Policy of Compactness and Quality', *Bulletin of Activities*, no. 27 (25 July 1961). See also 'The Combat Rules and Regulations of Our Army Are the Product of Mao Tse-tung's Military Thought', by the Military Science Academy, *Bulletin of Activities*, no. 29 (1 Aug 1961), *The Politics of the Chinese Red Army*, ed. J. Chester Cheng (Stanford, California: Stanford University, 1966) pp. 674–89, 729–35.

42. For discussion of such an Asian collective system, see for example Arthur S. Lall, 'The Political Effects of the Chinese Bomb', *Bulletin of the Atomic Scientists* (Feb 1967) p. 22; Donald Edward Kennedy, *The Security of Southern Asia* (New York: Frederick A. Praeger, 1965) p. 234.

43. See Alastair Buchan, 'An Asian Balance of Power', *Australian Journal of*

Politics and History, XII (Aug 1966), 278 ff.; Walter B. Wentz, *Nuclear Proliferation* (Washington: Public Affairs Press, 1968).

44. See Leonard Beaton, *Must the Bomb Spread?* (New York: Penguin, 1966) p. 57.

45. *New York Times*, 9 Jan 1965.

46. *New York Times*, 8 Sept 1968.

47. Leonard Beaton, *Must the Bomb Spread?*, p. 57.

48. 'News Digest: India Studying N-Weapons', News despatch from New Delhi, *Edmonton Journal*, 26 Jan 1970.

49. See Kiichi Saeki and Kai Wakaizumi, 'The Problems of Japan's Security', *China and the Peace of Asia*, ed. Alastair Buchan (New York: Frederick A. Praeger, 1965), 227.

50. *New York Times*, 1 Apr 1969.

51. 'Japan's Defence Budget up Sharply', news dispatch from Tokyo, *Edmonton Journal*, 26 Jan 1970.

52. 'Nixon's Vietnam Assessment', Joseph Alsop, Los Angeles Times Service, *Edmonton Journal*, 6 Mar 1969.

53. Alastair Buchan, *A World of Nuclear Power?*, p. 9.

54. Alastair Buchan, 'An Asian Balance of Power?', p. 279.

55. Quoted by Howard Margolis in his 'The Bomb in China', *Bulletin of the Atomic Scientists* (Dec 1964) p. 37.

56. See U.S. Atomic Energy Commission, *Foreign Atomic List* (1 Apr 1967).

57. Herman Kahn, *Thinking about the Unthinkable* (New York: Horizon Press, 1962) pp. 212–13.

58. *New York Times*, 16 Dec 1966.

59. *New York Times*, 28 Oct 1966.

60. *New York Times*, 18 June 1967.

61. See 'Statement by the U.S. Representative at the Geneva Conference', 19 Sept 1967, *U.S. Department of State Bulletin*, 57, no. 1478 (23 Oct 1967), 543–4. See also *Stopping the Spread of Nuclear Weapons*, p. 27.

62. 'Statement by the U.S. Representative at the Geneva Conference', p. 545. See also *New York Times*, 30 Jan 1970.

63. Ibid.

64. *Stopping the Spread of Nuclear Weapons*, p. 27.

CHAPTER 7

1. Such drastic changes could happen as a result of a civil war or similar events.

2. See 'Strategic Problems of China's Revolutionary War', *Selected Works*, I (New York: International Publishers, 1954) p. 180.

3. 'Statement by the Spokesman of the Chinese Government – A Comment on the Soviet Government's Statement of 21 August', 1 Sept 1963, in

People of the World, Unite, for the Complete, Thorough, Total and Resolute Pro-hibition and Destruction of Nuclear Weapons (Peking: Foreign Languages Press, 1963) p. 60.

4. See 'Long Live the Victory of People's War', *Peking Review* no. 36 (3 Sept 1965) 9–31.

5. Mao Tse-tung, 'Problems of Strategy in Guerilla War against Japan', May 1938, in *Selected Military Writings* (Peking: Foreign Languages Press, 1963) p. 155.

6. Mao Tse-tung, 'Problems of Strategy in China's Revolutionary War', *Selected Works*, I (Peking: Foreign Languages Press, 1965) 207.

7. *Comrade Mao Tse-tung on 'Imperialism and All Reactionaries Are Paper Tigers'* (Peking: Foreign Languages Press, 1958) p. 26. See also *Peking Review*, no. 36 (6 Sept 1963) 10.

8. Chou En-Lai, 'The Present International Situation and China's Foreign Policy', 10 Feb 1958, *NCNA*, 11 Feb 1958, in *Current Background*, no. 492 (14 Feb 1958) 1–13.

9. For a detailed analysis, see Alice Langley Hsieh, *Communist China's Strategy in the Nuclear Era* (Englewood Cliffs, N.J.: Prentice-Hall, 1962) pp. 84, 87–9, 121 and 91 ff. See also editorial, *People's Daily* and *Red Flag*, 6 Sept 1963, *Peking Review*, no. 37 (13 Sept 1963) 6–23.

10. *People's Daily*, 31 July 1963. See also *Peking Review*, no. 31 (2 Aug 1963) 7–8.

11. 'Defending the Motherland! . . .', iii.

12. Ibid., iii.

13. 'China Successfully Explodes Another Atom Bomb', *Hsinhua* (*NCNA*) dispatch, 14 May 1965. See also *Peking Review* (21 May 1965).

14. 'China Successfully Conducts Nuclear Explosion Containing Thermo-Nuclear Material', *Hsinhua* (*NCNA*) dispatch, 9 May 1966, See also *Peking Review*, 13 May 1966.

15. *Peking Review*, no. 21 (20 May 1966) 8. See also *New York Times*, 10 May 1966.

16. 'China Successfully Conducted Guided Missile – Nuclear Weapon Test', *Hsinhua* (*NCNA*) dispatch 27 Oct 1966. See also *Peking Review*, 28 Oct 1966).

17. See *New York Times*, 4 Nov 1966.

18. Ibid.

19. 'China Successfully Conducts New Nuclear Explosion', *Hsinhua* (*NCNA*) dispatch, 28 Dec 1966. See also *Peking Review*, 1 Jan 1967.

20. 'China's First Hydrogen Bomb Successfully Exploded', *Hsinhua* (*NCNA*) dispatch, 17 June 1967. See also *Peking Review*, 23 June 1967.

21. *Hsinhua* (*NCNA*) dispatch, 28 Dec 1968.

2. Ibid.

23. 'China Victoriously Conducts a New Hydrogen Bomb Explosion, Successfully Conducts the First Underground Nuclear Test', *Hsinhua* (*NCNA*) dispatch, 4 Oct 1969. See also *Peking Review*, 10 Oct 1969.

24. 'Japanese Reactionaries Feverishly Push Policy of Armaments Expansion and War Preparations', *Peking Review*, no. 47 (21 Nov 1969) 28. As mentioned earlier, owing to the nature of space satellites, Communist China did not mention their military and political implications after her 1970 and 1971 tests.

25. For example, a modest nuclear force with its own delivery system would on average cost $230–310 million a year. For details, see Leonard Beaton, *Must the Bomb Spread?* pp. 30–1. See also his 'Capabilities of Non-Nuclear Powers', in *A World of Nuclear Power?*, ed. A Buchan, 32 ff. In 1966, Glenn T. Seaborg, Chairman of the U.S. Atomic Energy Commission, estimated that an initial nuclear programme would cost a country less advanced than India about 50–100 million dollars; see *New York Times*, 2 Mar 1966.

26. For further discussion of these treaties, see Edwin Brown Firmage, 'The Treaty on the Non-proliferation of Nuclear Weapons', *American Journal of International Law*, 63, no. 4 (Oct 1969) 711–46.

27. See U.S. Atomic Energy Commission, *Foreign Reactor List* (1 Apr 1967).

28. Ibid.

29. U.S. Congress Joint Committee on Atomic Energy, *Nonproliferation of Nuclear Weapons*, Hearings before the Joint Committee on Atomic Energy, Congress of the United States, Eighty-ninth Congress, Second Session, in S. Res. 179, 23 Feb and 1 and 7 Mar 1966 (Washington: U.S. Government Printing Office, 1966) p. 79.

30. William C. Foster, 'Risks of Nuclear Proliferation: New Direction in Arms Control and Disarmament', *Foreign Affairs*, 43 (1964–5) 590.

31. H. A. Kissinger, *The Necessity for Choice* (New York : Harper, 1961) p. 242.

32. Herman Kahn, *Thinking about the Unthinkable* (New York: Horizon Press, 1962) p. 214.

33. Many writers, including Hans J. Morgenthau and Leonard Beaton, also recognized this danger. See Hans J. Morgenthau, 'Has Atomic War Really Become Impossible?', *Bulletin of the Atomic Scientists* (Jan 1956) p. 7–9; Leonard Beaton, *Must the Bomb Spread?* 32 ff.

34. Stanley Hoffman, 'Nuclear Proliferation and World Politics', p. 107.

35. Raymond Aron, *The Great Debate*, p. 62.

36. See Chapter 5 above.

37. *NCNA*, Cairo, 13 Jan 1965, in *Survey on China Mainland Press*, No. 3380.

38. *New York Times*, 9 Apr 1965.

39. Sisir Gupta, 'The Indian Dilemma', *A World of Nuclear Power?*, ed. Alastair Buchan, p. 61.

40. Hans J. Morgenthau, 'Alliance in Theory and Practice', *Alliance Policy in the Cold War* (Baltimore: The Johns Hopkins University Press, 1959) pp. 184–212.

41. R. C. Snyder, *Deterrence, Weapons Systems and Decision-Making* (China Lake, Calif.: U.S. Naval Ordnance Station, 1961) p. 70.

42. Francis O. Wilcox, 'The Nonaligned States and the United Nations', *Neutralism and Nonalignment*, ed. Laurence W. Martin (New York: Frederick A. Praeger, 1962) p. 123.

43. Cit. John Silard, 'Nuclear Weapons: A Liability', *Bulletin of the Atomic Scientists* (Sept 1966) p. 18.

Select Bibliography

Books

Armbruster, Frank E., *China Briefing* (Chicago: University of Chicago Press, 1968).

Aron, Raymond, *The Great Debate* (Garden City, New York: Doubleday, 1965).

Barnett, A. Doak, *Communist China and Asia: A Challenge to American Policy* (New York: Random House, 1960).

Beaton, Leonard, *Must the Bomb Spread?* (New York: Penguin, 1966).

— and John Maddox, *The Spread of Nuclear Weapons* (New York: Frederick A. Praeger, 1962).

Break the Nuclear Monopoly, Eliminate Nuclear Weapons (Peking: Foreign Languages Press, 1965).

Brodie, Bernard, *Escalation and the Nuclear Option* (Princeton, N. J.: Princeton University Press, 1966).

Buchan, Alastair (ed.) *China and the Peace of Asia* (New York: Frederick A. Praeger, 1965).

— (ed.) *A World of Nuclear Powers?* (Englewood Cliffs, N.J.: Prentice-Hall, 1966).

Cheng, J. Chester (ed.), *The Politics of the Chinese Red Army* (Stanford, Calif.: The Hoover Institution on War, Revolution and Peace, 1966).

Clemens, W. C., *The Arms Race and Sino-Soviet Relations* (Stanford, Calif.: Hoover Institution, 1968).

Dutt, Vidya Prakash, *China and the World: An Analysis of Communist China's Foreign Policy* (New York: Frederick A. Praeger, 1966).

Fiscal Year 1971 – Defense Program and Budget (statement by Secretary of Defense Melvin R. Laird, 20 Feb 1970) (Washington: U.S. Government Printing Office, 1970).

Fitzgerald, C. P., *The Chinese View of Their Place in the World* (Oxford: Oxford University Press, 1964).

Gareau, Frederick H. (ed.), *The Balance of Power and Nuclear Deterrence* (Boston, Mass.: Houghton Mifflin, 1962).

Griffith, William E., *The Sino-Soviet Rift* (Cambridge, Mass.: The M.I.T. Press, 1963).

107

Halperin, Morton H., *China and the Bomb* (New York: Frederick A. Praeger, 1965).

— *China and Nuclear Proliferation* (Chicago: University of Chicago Press, 1966).

— *Chinese Nuclear Strategy: the Early Post-Detonation Period* (London: Institute for Strategic Studies, 1965.

— *Is China Turning in?* (Cambridge, Mass.: Harvard University, 1965).

— and Dwight H. Perkins, *Communist China and Arms Control* (Cambridge, Mass.: Harvard University, 1965).

Hearings before the Subcommittee of the Committee on Appropriations, House of Representatives, 91st Congress, First Session (Washington: U.S. Government Printing Office, 1969).

Hinton, Harold C., *Communist China in World Politics* (Boston: Houghton Mifflin, 1966).

— *Communist China's External Policy and Behavior as A Nuclear Power* (Arlington, Va.: Institute for Defense Analyses, 1963).

Ho Ping-ti and Tang Tsou (eds), *China in Crisis: China's Heritage and the Communist Political System*, vol. 1 (Chicago: University of Chicago Press, 1968).

Hoffman, Stanley, *Contemporary Theory in International Relations* (Englewood Cliffs, N.J.: Prentice-Hall, 1960).

— *The State of War: Essays in the Theory and Practice of International Politics* (New York: Frederick A. Praeger, 1965).

Hsieh, Alice Langley, *Communist China and Nuclear Force* (Santa Monica, Calif.: Rand Corp., 1963).

— *Communist China's Military Doctrine and Strategy* (Santa Monica, Calif.: Rand Corp., 1964).

— *Communist China's Strategy in the Nuclear Era* (Englewood Cliffs, N.J.: Prentice-Hall, 1962).

— *Foreword to the Japanese Edition of Communist China's Strategy in the Nuclear Era* (Santa Monica, Calif.: Rand Corp., 1965).

Institute for Strategic Studies, *The Military Balance 1970–1971* (London, 1970).

— *Strategic Survey 1970* (London, 1971).

Kahn, Herman, *Thinking about the Unthinkable* (New York: Horizon Press, 1962).

Kaplan, Morton A., *System and Process in International Politics* (New York: John Wiley & Sons, 1964).

Kennedy, Donald Edward, *The Security of Southern Asia* (New York: Frederick A. Praeger, 1965).

Larus, Joel, *Nuclear Weapons Safety and the Common Defense* (Columbus, Ohio: Ohio State University Press, 1967).

Levi, Werner, *Fundamentals of World Organization* (Minneapolis, Minn.: The University of Minnesota Press, 1950).

Maddox, John: see Beaton above.

Morgenthau, Hans J., *Politics among Nations: The Struggle for Power and Peace* (New York: Alfred A. Knopf, 1967).

The Nonproliferation of Nuclear Weapons (Washington: U.S. Government Printing Office, 1968).

People of the World, Unite, for the Complete, Thorough, Total and Resolute Prohibition and Destruction of Nuclear Weapons (Peking: Foreign Languages Press, 1963).

Rosecrance, R. N. (ed.), *The Dispersion of Nuclear Weapons: Strategy and Politics* (New York: Columbia University Press, 1964).

— *Problems of Nuclear Proliferation* (Los Angeles: University of California, 1966).

Rosenau, James N., *International Politics and Foreign Policy: A Reader in Research and Theory* (New York: Free Press of Glencoe, 1961).

Rothstein, Robert L., *On Nuclear Proliferation* (New York: School of International Affairs, Columbia University, 1966).

Ryan, W. L., and S. Summerlin, *China Cloud: America's Tragedy and China's Rise to Nuclear Power* (Boston: Little, Brown, 1968).

Schelling, Thomas C., *The Strategy of Conflict* (New York: Oxford University Press, 1963).

Stopping the Spread of Nuclear Weapons (New York: U.N.A.–U.S.A., 1967).

Tsou Tang (ed.), *China in Crisis: China's Policies in Asia and America's Alternatives*, vol. 2 (Chicago: University of Chicago Press, 1968).

U.S. Congress: Joint Committee on Atomic Energy, *Impact of Chinese Communist Nuclear Weapons Program on U.S. National Security* (Washington: U.S. Government Printing Office, 1967).

U.S. Congress: Joint Committee on Atomic Energy, *Nonproliferation of Nuclear Weapons* (Washington: U.S. Government Printing Office, 1966.

U.S. Congress: Senate, *U.S. Policy with Respect to Mainland China* (Washington: U.S. Government Printing Office, 1966.

Wint, Guy, *Communist China's Crusade: Mao's Road to Power and the New Campaign for World Revolution* (New York: Praeger, 1965).

Articles

Abelson, Philip H., 'The Chinese A-Bomb', *Air Force Magazine* (Jan 1965), p. 35.

Ali, S. M., 'China's Bomb and After', *Far Eastern Economic Review* no. 48 (24 June 1965) 610–15.

Augenstein, B. W., 'The Chinese and French Programs for the Development of National Nuclear Forces', *Orbis*, XI no. 3 (fall 1967) 846–63.

Baum, Richard, 'China: Year of the Mangoes', *Asian Survey*, IX no. 1 (Jan 1969) 1–17.

Beaton, Leonard, 'I.S.S. [Institute for Strategic Studies] View', *Survival* (Jan–Feb 1965) pp. 2–4.

Bechhoefer, Bernhard G., 'The Test-Ban Treaty: Some Further Considerations', *Bulletin of the Atomic Scientists* (May 1964) pp. 25–7.

Bell, Coral, 'Security in Asia: Reappraisals after Vietnam', *International Journal*, XXIV no. 1 (winter 1968–9) 1–12.

Bobrow, David, 'Realism about Nuclear Spread', *Bulletin of the Atomic Scientists* (Dec 1965) 20–2.

Bowman, Richard C., 'The Chinese Bomb: Its Military–Political Implications', *Air Force and Space Digest*, no. 48 (Jan 1965) 32–4.

Boyd, R. G., 'The New Chinese Policy', *International Journal*, xxiv no. 1 (winter 1968–9) 86–108.

Buchan, Alastair, 'An Asian Balance of Power', *Australian Journal of Politics and History*, xii no. 2 (Aug 1966) 271–81.

Candlin, A. H. S., 'The Chinese Nuclear Threat', *Army Quarterly* (Apr 1966) 50–60.

Carlisle, Donald S., 'The Sino-Soviet Schism', *Orbis*, viii no. 4 (winter 1965) 790–815.

Chang Hu, 'A General Study of the Relations between the Chinese and the Laotian Communists', *Chinese Communist Affairs Monthly*, vol. 12, no. 9 (1 Nov 1969) 35–7.

'Relationship between the Chinese Communists and Nepal', *Chinese Communist Affairs Monthly*, vol. 12, no. 7 (1 Sept 1969) 52–3.

Chang Tung-tsai, 'Japan and Peiping's Nuclear Explosion', *Wen-ti yi yuan-chu*, vol. 5, no. 9 (June 1966) 34–36.

Ching Yi-hung, 'Mao's Nuclear Base and Prospects', *Free China Review* (July 1966) pp. 34–8.

Chiu, Hungdah, "Communist China's Attitude Towards Nuclear Test', *China Quarterly*, no. 21 (Jan–Mar 1965) 96–107.

Clemens, Walter C., Jr., 'Chinese Nuclear Tests: Trends and Portents', *China Quarterly*, no. 32 (Oct–Dec 1967) 111–31.

Coffey, Rosemary Klineberg, 'The Chinese and Ballistic Missile Defense', *Bulletin of the Atomic Scientists* (Dec 1965) pp. 17–19.

Davis, Paul C., 'The Coming Chinese Communist Nuclear Threat and U.S. Sea-Based A.B.M. Options', *Orbis*, xi no. 1 (spring 1967) 45–79.

Deutsch, Karl W., and J. David Singer, 'Multipolar Power Systems and International Stability', *World Politics*, vol. 16, no. 3 (Apr 1964) 390–406.

'Discussion of Chinese Nuclear Weapons Development', *Bulletin of the Atomic Scientists* (Apr 1966) pp. 29–30.

Elegant, Robert S., 'China's Next Phase', *Foreign Affairs* (Oct 1967) 137–50.

Fairbank, John K., 'China's World Order', *Encounter*, vol. 27 (Dec 1966) 14–15.

'The People's Middle Kingdom', *Foreign Affairs* (July 1966) 574–86.

Fei Yuan, 'Peiping–Moscow New Struggle and Chinese Communist Nuclear Blackmail', *Wen-ti yi yuan-chu*, vol. 4, no. 2 (Nov 1964) 28–34. ,

Feld, Bernard T., 'After the Nonproliferation Treaty – What Next?', *Bulletin of the Atomic Scientists*, (Sept 1968) pp. 2–3.

'The Nonproliferation of Nuclear Weapons', *Bulletin of the Atomic Scientists* (Dec 1964) pp. 2–6.

'On the Chinese Separation Technology', *Bulletin of the Atomic Scientists* (Sept 1966) pp. 33–4.

'A Pledge: No First Use', *Bulletin of the Atomic Scientists* (May 1967) pp. 46–8.

'To Be Nuclear or Not', *Bulletin of the Atomic Scientists* (May 1967).

Fisher, Roger, 'Perceiving the World through Bipolar Glasses', *Daedalus*, vol. 93, 910–15.

Fitzgerald, C. P., 'The Directions of (Chinese) Foreign Policy', *Bulletin of the Atomic Scientists* (June 1966) pp. 65–70.

'[Chinese] Foreign Policy: A Revolutionary Hiatus', *Bulletin of the Atomic Scientists* (Feb 1969) pp. 53–60.

Fix, Joseph E., III, 'China – the Nuclear Threat', *Air University Quarterly Review* (Mar–Apr 1966) pp. 28–39.

Foster, William C., 'Risks of Nuclear Proliferation: New Direction in Arms Control and Disarmament', *Foreign Affairs* (July 1965) 588–601.

Forty-second (The) Anniversary of Founding of Chinese People's Liberation Army Warmly Celebrated – Speech by Chief of General Staff Huang Yung-sheng', *Peking Review*, no. 32 (6 Aug 1969) 7–9.

Frank, Lewis A., 'Nuclear Weapons Development in China', *Bulletin of the Atomic Scientists* (Jan 1966) pp. 12–15.

Garthoff, Raymond L., 'A Soviet Critique of China's "Total Strategy" ', *The Reporter*, XXXIV no. 10 (19 May 1966) 48–49.

'Great Achievements of China's Nuclear Testing', *Survey of China Mainland Press*, no. 4094 (8 Jan 1968).

Griffith, Samuel B., 'Communist China's Capacity to Make War', *Foreign Affairs* (Jan 1965) pp. 217–36.

Guillain, Robert, 'Ten Years of (Chinese nuclear) Secrecy', *Bulletin of the Atomic Scientists* (Feb 1967) pp. 24–5.

Hall, John A., 'Risks of Nuclear Proliferation: Atoms for Peace, or War', *Foreign Affairs* (July 1965).

Halperin, Morton H., 'China and the Bomb – Chinese Nuclear Strategy', *China Quarterly*, no. 21 (Jan–Mar 1965) 74–86.

— 'Chinese Attitudes toward the Use and Control of Nuclear Weapons', *China in Crisis*, vol. 2, 135–57.

— 'Chinese Nuclear Strategy: the Early Post-Detonation Period', *Asian Survey*, vol. 5, no. 6 (June 1965) 271–8.

Halpern, A. M., 'China in the Postwar World', *China Quarterly*, no. 21 (Jan–Mar 1965) 20–45.

Hanrieder, Wolfram F., 'The International System: Bipolar or Multipolar', *Journal of Conflict Resolution*, vol. 9 (1965) 299–308.

Harris, William R., 'Chinese Nuclear Doctrine: The Decade Prior to Weapons Development (1945–55)', *China Quarterly*, no. 21 (Jan–Mar 1965) 87–95.

Harrison, Stanley L., 'Nth Nation Challenges: the Present Perspective', *Orbis*, IX no. 1 (spring 1965) 155–70.

'Heavy Blow to Nuclear Monopoly of U.S. Imperialism and Social-Imperialism', *Peking Review*, no. 47 (21 Nov 1969) 18–21.

Henri, Ernst, 'Mao Tse-tung Gazes upon Five Continents', *Atlas*, vol. 14 (Dec 1967) 14–15.

Hsieh, Alice Langley, 'China's Secret Military Paper: Military Doctrine and Strategy', *China Quarterly*, no. 18 (Apr–June 1964) 79–99.

— 'Communist China and Nuclear Warfare', *China Quarterly*, no. 2 (Apr–June 1960) 1–12.

— 'Sino-Soviet Nuclear Dialogue', *Bulletin of the Atomic Scientists* (Jan 1965) pp. 16–21.

Hudson, G., 'Paper Tigers and Nuclear Teeth', *China Quarterly*, no. 39 (July–Sept 1969), 64–75.

Iklé, F. C., 'Nth Countries and Disarmament', *Bulletin of the Atomic Scientists* (Dec 1960) pp. 391–394.

Inglis, David R., 'The Chinese Bombshell', *Bulletin of the Atomic Scientists* (Feb 1965) pp. 19–21.

'Missile Defense, Nuclear Spread and Vietnam', *Bulletin of the Atomic Scientists* (May 1967) pp. 49–52.

'Intensified U.S.–Soviet Collaboration against China: Essence of So-called Preliminary Talks on "Strategic Arms Limitation",' *Peking Review*, no. 46 (14 Nov 1969) 28.

'Is Red China's H-Bomb a Product of the West?', *Atlas*, vol. 16 (Dec 1968) 22–4.

Kalicki, J. H., 'China, America, and Arms Control', *The World Today* (Apr 1970) 147–55.

Lall, Arthur S., 'The Political Effects of the Chinese Bomb', *Bulletin of the Atomic Scientists* (Feb 1965) pp. 21–4.

'Mainland China and U.S. Security', *Bulletin of the Atomic Scientists* (Apr 1964) pp. 24–27.

Levi, Werner, 'The Future of South-east Asia', *Asian Survey*, x no. 4 (Apr 1970) 348–57.

'Long Live the Victory of People's War', *People's Daily*, 2 Sept 1965, *Peking Review* (3 Sept 1965) pp. 9–30.

'Report to the Ninth National Congress of the Communist Party of China', *Peking Review*, no. 18 (30 Apr 1969) 16–35.

Lindbeck, John, 'An Isolationist (Chinese) Science Policy', *Bulletin of the Atomic Scientists* (Feb 1969) pp. 66–72.

Lo Shih-fu, 'Chinese Communist Thrust into South-east Asia', *Issues & Studies*, xi no. 1 (Oct 1969) 37–42.

'The Paris Talks and Peiping's Policy of Southward Expansion', *Wen-ti yi yuan-chu*, vol. 8, no. 6 (Mar 1969) 18–21.

'Strategic and Tactical Problems of the Laotian Communists', *Issues & Studies*, vi no. 4 (Jan 1970) 39–49.

Lu Yung-shu, 'Chinese Communist Nuclear Tests Viewed after the Eighth Blast', *Issues & Studies*, v no. 5 (Feb 1969) 1–6.

Mackintosh, Malcolm, 'The Military Aspects of the Sino-Soviet Dispute', *Bulletin of the Atomic Scientists* (Oct 1965) pp. 16–17.

McMorris, S. Carter, 'World Peace and the Bombs of China', *The Midwest Quarterly*, ix no. 1 (Oct 1967) 53–64.

Maddox, John 'Prestige Unimportant', *Bulletin of the Atomic Scientists* (May 1967) pp. 63.

Margolis, Howard, 'The Bomb in China', *Bulletin of the Atomic Scientists* (Dec 1964) pp. 36–39.

Masani, M. R., 'The Challenge of the Chinese Bomb – ii', *India Quarterly* xxi no. 1 (Jan–Mar 1965) 15–28.

Matsumara, Tomokatsu, 'How Likely a Head-on Collision?', *Atlas*, vol. 15, no. 2 (Feb 1968) 36–8.

Melby, John F., 'The Cold War – Second Phase: China', *International Journal*, xx no. 3 (summer 1968) 421–34.

'Missions of National Liberation Organizations and Foreign Friends in China: Great China's Successful Guided Nuclear Missile Test', *Survey of Mainland China Press*, no. 3819 (7 Nov 1966).

Morgenthau, Hans J., 'Has Atomic War Really Become Impossible?', *Bulletin of the Atomic Scientists* (Jan 1956) pp. 7–9.

A New Foreign Policy for the United States: Basic Issues', *Bulletin of the Atomic Scientists* (Jan 1967) pp. 7–11.

'The United States and China', *China in Crisis*, vol. 2, 93–105.

'The Vietnam Crisis and China', *Bulletin of the Atomic Scientists* (June 1965) p. 27.

Murphey, Rhoads, 'China and the Dominoes', *Asian Survey*. xi no. 9 (Sept 1966), 510–15.

Nehru, R. K., 'The Challenge of the Chinese Bomb – I', *India Quarterly*, xxi no. 1 (Jan–Mar 1965) 3–14.

Oldham, C. H. G., 'Science Travels the Mao Road', *Bulletin of the Atomic Scientists* (Feb 1969) pp. 80–3.

'Origin [The] and Development of the Differences between the Leadership of the C.P.S.U. and Ourselves – Comment on the Open Letter of the Central Committee of the C.P.S.U.', editorial, *People's Daily* in *Peking Review*, no. 37 (13 Sept 1963) 6–23.

Palmer, Norman D., 'The Defense of South Asia', *Orbis*, ix no. 4 (winter 1966) 898–929.

Pao Chin-an, 'Peiping's Capacity for Nuclear Weaponry, *Communist Chinese Affairs: A Bi-Monthly Review*, vol. 5, no. 2 (Apr 1968) 10–14.

Patil, R. L. M., 'China and Nuclear Proliferation', *China Report*, iv no. 1 (Jan–Feb 1969), 4–6.

'Peiping Supports Thai "People's Liberation Army"', *Facts & Features*, ii no. 9 (19 Feb 1969) 4–6.

'Peiping's Recent Nuclear Detonations: Their Technical and Political Implications', *Issues & Studies*, vi no. 2 (Nov 1969) 4–6.

'A Plea for People's War: Peking's Manifesto for World Revolution', editorial, *Current Scene*, iii no. 28 (1 Oct 1965) 1–10.

Powell, R. L., 'Great Powers and Atomic Bombs are "Paper Tigers"', *China Quarterly*, no. 23 (July–Sept 1965) 55–63.

Powell, R. L., 'Risks of Nuclear Proliferation – China's Bomb: Exploition and Reactions', *Foreign Affairs* (July 1965) pp. 616–25.

Pye, Lucian W., 'Coming Dilemmas for China's Leaders', *Foreign Affairs* (Apr 1966) pp. 387–402.

Rosecrance, R. N., 'Bipolarity, Multipolarity and the Future', *Journal of Conflict Resolution*, vol. 10, no. 3 (Sept 1966) 314–27.

Rothstein, R. L., 'Nuclear Proliferation and American Policy', *Political Science Quarterly*, vol. 82 (Mar 1967) 14–34.

Ruina, J. P., 'The Nuclear Arms Race: Diagnosis and Treatment', *Bulletin of the Atomic Scientists* (Oct 1968) pp. 19–22.

'Rusk and Bundy Interviewed on Red China's Nuclear Testing', *Department of State Bulletin* (2 Nov 1964) pp. 614–17.

'Scientific Research in China', *Bulletin of the Atomic Scientists* (May 1966) pp. 36–43.

'Secretary (Rusk) Discusses Mainland China in Television Interview', *Department of State Bulletin* (30 Nov 1964) pp. 771–2.

Smith, Bruce L. R., 'The Non-proliferation Treaty and East–West Détente', *Journal of International Affairs*, XXII no. 1 (1968) 89–106.

'Source Material: Several Important Problems concerning the Current International Situation', *Bulletin of Activities*, no. 17 (25 Apr 1961), in *The Politics of the Chinese Red Army*, ed. J. Chester Cheng (Stanford, Calif.: The Hoover Institution on War, Revolution and Peace, 1966) pp. 480–7.

'Statement of the Chinese Government Advocating the Complete, Thorough, Total and Resolute Prohibition and Destruction of Nuclear Weapons (and) Proposing a Conference of the Government Heads of All Countries of the World', 31 July 1963, *Peking Review*, no. 31 (2 Aug 1963) 7–8.

Stone, Jeremy J., 'On Proliferation: Where's the Danger?', *Bulletin of the Atomic Scientists* (Nov 1965) pp. 15–18.

'A study of Peiping's Eighth Nuclear Test', *Facts & Features*, II no. 7 (22 Jan 1969) 4–6.

Tan Shi-sen, 'Focal Point of Mao–Khrushchev Struggle', *Wen-ti yi yaun-chu*, vol. 4, no. 1 (Oct 1964) 1–2.

Tao Lung-sheng, 'From the Treaty for a Partial Nuclear Test Ban to the Anti-Proliferation Treaty', *Wen-ti yi yuan -chu*, vol. 7, no. 7 (Apr 1968) 33–5. Thirring, Hans, 'Can We Sleep Soundly in the Shadow of the Hydrogen Bomb?', *Bulletin of the Atomic Scientists* (Feb 1955) pp. 145–52.

Thornton, Thomas P., 'Communist China and Nuclear Weapons', *Military Review* (Sept 1964) pp. 31–8.

Tretiak, Daniel, 'Changes in Chinese Attention to South-east Asia, –1967 1969', *Current Scene*, VII no. 21 (1 Nov 1969) 1–17

Tsou, Tang, and M. H. Halperin, 'Mao Tse-tung's Revolutionary Strategy and Peking's International Behavior', *American Political Science Review*, vol. 59, no. 1 (Mar 1965) 80–99.

Tsui Chui-yen, 'Peiping's Design in Exploding Its Nuclear Device', *Issues & Studies*, vol. 1, no. 6 (Mar 1965) 10–20.

'Two Different Lines on the Question of War and Peace – Comment on the Open Letter of the Central Committee of the C.P.S.U. (5), *People's Daily* and *Red Flag*, editorial, *Peking Review*, no. 47 (27 Nov 1963) 6–16.

'U.N. Political Committee Approves "Nuclear Non-Proliferation" Treaty under U.S.–Soviet Manipulation', *Survey of China Mainland Press*, no. 4200 (18 Jan 1968).

'U.S. Imperialism's Feverish Speed-up of Nuclear Arms Drive for War', *Peking Review*, no. 8 (20 Feb 1970) 28.

Valkenier, Elizabeth Kridl, 'Changing Soviet Perspectives on the Liberation Revolution', *Orbis*, IX no. 4 (winter 1966) 953–69.

Waltz, Kenneth N., 'The Stability of a Bipolar World', *Daedalus*, vol. 93 (1964) 881–909.

Whiting, Allen Shess, 'Foreign Policy of Communist China', *Foreign Policy in World Politics,* ed. Roy C. Macridis (Englewood Cliffs, N.J.: Prentice-Hall, 1967) pp. 267–90.

Wilcox, Wayne, 'The Prospective Politics of Insecurity and Strategic Asymmetry in Asia', *International Journal,* XXIV no. 1 (winter 1968–9) 13–34.

Willrich, Mason, 'No First Use of Nuclear Weapons: An Assessment', *Orbis,* IX no. 2 (summer 1965) 299–315.

'World Reactions to the Chinese Nuclear Bomb', *Foreign Affairs Reports,* vol. 14, no. 1 (Jan 1965) 3–14.

Wu Chi-Fang, 'Peiping's Nuclear Test and Its Military Industry', *Chinese Communist Affairs,* vol. 2, no. 1 (Feb 1965) 13–18 (bi-monthly).

Yahuda, Michael B., 'China's Nuclear Option', *Bulletin of the Atomic Scientists* (Feb 1969) pp. 72–77.

— 'China's Nuclear Policy', *The Year Book of World Affairs 1969,* pp. 38–52.

— 'Chinese Foreign Policy after 1963: the Maoist Phases', *China Quarterly,* no. 36 (Oct–Dec 1968) 93–113.

Yin Ching-Yao, 'Hanoi-Peiping-Moscow', *Wen-ti yi yuan-chu,* vol. 6, no. 6 (Mar 1967) 44–9.

Young, Elizabeth, 'The Nonproliferation Treaty: An Acceptable Balance', *Bulletin of the Atomic Scientists* (Nov 1967) pp. 37–8.

Young, Oran R., 'Chinese Views on the Spread of Nuclear Weapons', *China Quarterly,* no. 26 (Apr–June 1966), 136–70.

Yuter, S. C., 'Preventing Nuclear Proliferation through the Legal Control of China's Bomb', *Orbis,* XII no. 4 (winter 1969) 1018–41.

Other sources

China Report, India, 1964–71.
Chinese Communist Affairs Bi-monthly, Taipei, 1964–71.
Chung-Yang Jih-Pao (Central Daily), Taipei, 1964–71.
Current Scene: Development in Mainland China, Hong Kong, 1964–71.
Facts & Features, Taipei, 1964–71.
Fei-Ching Yüeh-Pao (Chinese Communist Affairs Monthly), Taipei, 1964–71.
Hung Ch'i (Red Flag), Peking (or Peiping), 1964–71.
Issues & Studies: A Monthly Journal of Communist Problems and World Affairs, Taipei, 1964–71.
Jen-Min Jih-Pao (People's Daily), Peking, 1964–71.
Kwan-Ming Jih-Pao (Kwan-Ming Daily), Peking, 1964–71.
New York Times, 1964–71.
Peking Review, Peking, 1964–71.
Survey of China Mainland Press, Hong Kong, 1964–71.

Index